MW01119682

Disability and Justice

Disability and Justice

The Capabilities Approach in Practice

Christopher A. Riddle

LEXINGTON BOOKS
Lanham • Boulder • New York • Toronto • Plymouth, UK

Published by Lexington Books
A wholly owned subsidary of Rowman & Littlefield
4501 Forbes Boulevard, Suite 200, Lanham, Maryland 20706
www.rowman.com

10 Thornbury Road, Plymouth PL6 7PP, United Kingdom

British Library Cataloguing in Publication Information Available

Library of Congress Cataloging-in-Publication Data
Library of Congress Cataloging-in-Publication Data Available
ISBN 978-0-7391-7802-7 (cloth: alk. paper)—ISBN 978-0-7391-7803-4 (electronic)

♾™ The paper used in this publication meets the minimum requirements of American
National Standard for Information Sciences—Permanence of Paper for Printed Library
Materials, ANSI/NISO Z39.48-1992.

Printed in the United States of America

For Norma & in memory of Larry
with love & appreciation

.

Contents

Figures

Foreword

Jerome E. Bickenbach

Christopher Riddle, in this admirable book, addresses the concern that traditional views of justice have, in some ways like society in general, marginalized people with disabilities, treating them, as John Rawls in his *Theory of Justice* explicitly did, as a special case to return to, once a theory has been developed.[1] As I remarked some years ago,[2] on its face the most exciting and potentially fruitful tactic to remedy this situation is to apply the powerful Capabilities Approach of economist-philosopher Amartya Sen and philosopher Martha Nussbaum to disability to fully integrate disability into the mainstream of egalitarian accounts of justice. The intuitive underpinning of this belief was simple enough: whatever else it is, disability is primarily a limitation—whether caused by impairments or by socially constructed impediments, or as I now believe the outcome of the interaction of the two[3]— in what a person can do or become, a limitation, that is, of the individual's capability.

I appreciated, as many disability scholars did, that all of this depends on consensus about the concept of disability itself, an issue over which there was persistent, and intransient debate: is disability fundamentally a decrement in health (the primary focus of health professionals) or social disadvantage (the primary focus of legal and political remedy)? Again, I and many others, hold that disability is an outcome of an interaction and that to deny the impact either of health determinants or social and environmental determinants is to fundamentally misconstrue the complex phenomenon that is disability. But however important the conceptualization of disability is, and despite the vast literature, much of it, sadly, is ideologically fraught and repetitive and, as Riddle shows, conceptual clarification is but the first step

ix

to operationalization and integration into a robust and workable theory of egalitarian justice that does justice to disability.

The theoretical attractiveness of the Capability Approach must always be offset by a critical examination of the approach in practice. Riddle agrees and addresses two substantial concerns. The first is the necessity in practice of moving from discrete assessments of the extent of functioning (in Sen's sense) that a person enjoys in one domain of life, to a cross-domain, summary measure of functioning. This is required in order to assess the social needs of persons with disabilities—resources or opportunities—needs the satisfaction of which would further egalitarian justice. Here there appear to be three distinct approaches: either identify a single domain, say health, and measure its achievement as a proxy for all capabilities (an approach taken by Venkatapuram[4]); or assemble assessments of need from several life domains and create a summation algorithm that combines these disparate measures (the approach of Wolff and De-Shalit[5]); or, finally use nonclassical test theories, such as Item Response or Rasch analysis, to create from existing data a single metric of functioning in terms of which needs can be cardinally measured. This last approach requires a huge body of comparable data, across functioning domains, a database that is simply not available, and Riddle does not pursue this option. Rejecting the first option, and finding, by means of an ingenious argument, the second unfeasible, Riddle concludes that the capability approach hits a practical roadblock at this point. Riddle then turns to the second concern that involves the familiar policy conundrum of how policy-makers can address inequalities of need, assuming for the sake of the argument that these needs can be assessed, without stigmatizing this population as "special." Acknowledging this concern, Riddle argues that, at a minimum, the Capability Approach is more "stigma-sensitive" than its competitors.

Riddle is very clear in this book that his critiques are constructive, in that they point to refinements and augmentations that can strengthen the Capability Approach and its application to disability. His suggested refinements—which build on the argument of Norman Daniels that health has a special moral significance,[6] as well as the Wolff and De-Shalit conception of "disadvantage"—are ingenious and sophisticated and clearly and boldly advance the discussion in what, I believe, will be a fruitful direction. His contribution is not just as a matter of philosophical elegance, it is also a contribution to the practical applicability to policy of the Capability Approach to help to achieve the goals and aspirations of the United Nations Convention on the Rights of Persons with Disabilities, namely the full social inclusion and participation of people with disabilities, on an equal basis with others.

Notes

1. John Rawls, *A Theory of Justice* (Cambridge: Harvard University Press, 1971).

2. Jerome Bickenbach, *Physical Disability and Social Policy* (Toronto: University of Toronto Press, 1993).

3. Jerome Bickenbach, *Ethics, Law, and Policy* (New York: Sage Publications, 2012).

4. Sridhar Venkatapuram, *Health Justice: An Argument from the Capabilities Approach* (Cambridge: Polity Press, 2011).

5. Jonathan Wolff and Avner De-Shalit, *Disadvantage* (Oxford: Oxford University Press, 2007).

6. Norman Daniels, *Just Health: Meeting Health Needs Fairly* (New York: Cambridge University Press, 2008).

Preface

I was first exposed to discussions of justice and disability in the winter of 2004 when taking a senior undergraduate seminar at Queen's University at Kingston, titled "The Philosophy of Law," under Jerome Bickenbach. This course was undoubtedly the undergraduate class that I took the most from. Under the guidance of Jerome Bickenbach and peers such as Christopher Lowry, I was exposed to how equality had been conceptualized before the law, and how our normative conceptions tended to exclude people with disabilities from the scope of justice.

What struck me as odd and unique about questioning how people with disabilities were being accommodated under our conceptions of justice was just how few people were doing it. It seemed to me to be such an obviously pressing topic that received either passing attention or none at all.

From that point forward, I have focused my academic attention on these and other related questions.

I would continue this work, at least tangentially, working on more policy-oriented questions during a Master of Arts degree at York University in Toronto during the 2005–2006 academic year. Here I benefited greatly from guidance from Lesley Jacobs, Geoffrey Reaume, and Marcia Rioux.

Despite having had some basic ideas about disability and justice for quite some time at this point, it was not until 2007 when I returned to Queen's University at Kingston that this project began to resemble what it is today. I would begin to study the Capabilities Approach more carefully and gain a finer understanding of what it purported to do for people with disabilities. The guidance I received while completing my PhD was more than I could have asked for.

Of course, Jerome Bickenbach was vital to my development. Without the educational opportunities he provided me I would not have a fraction of the knowledge I do now. I am tremendously indebted to him. Others were integral in my philosophical development during this time as well. Jackie

Davies, Colin Farrelly, Alistair Macleod, Adèle Mercier, Udo Schüklenk, Christine Sypnowich, and David Wasserman devoted countless hours to fine-tuning many aspects of this project and my reasoning.

During this time I also benefited from support from The Canadian Disability Policy Alliance, especially Mary Ann McColl and Mike Schaub.

While completing my PhD I also had the tremendous pleasure of benefiting from many of my peers' knowledge. François Boucher, Yual Chiek, Christine Esselmont, Omid Hejazi, Kyle Johannsen, Jim Molos, Nikoo Najand, Mark Rosner, Andrew D. F. Ross, Philip Shadd, and Katherine Wayne provided me many helpful comments throughout the process of formulating the ideas that would eventually be contained in this book.

I would also have a few wonderful opportunities that had a significant impact on this project. First, I was invited to Germany to the University of Tübingen to work with Martha Nussbaum. The time spent with her sharpening my critical remarks about the capabilities approach was invaluable.

Around this time I also benefited from critical comments on my work from Jennifer Prah Ruger.

Second, I was invited to the Swiss Paraplegic Research Institute, where I would continue to reformulate my thoughts and eventually develop my final critical remarks contained in this book. Here Sara Rubinelli stood out as being especially helpful.

I would eventually take an Assistant Professor position at Concordia University in Montreal and receive excellent mentoring from Matthew Barker, Murray Clarke, Andrea Falcon, Matthias Fritsch, Sheila Mason, David Morris, and Justin Smith. Unbeknownst to the students in my "Marxism," "Political Philosophy," and "Advanced Political Philosophy" seminars, much inspiration was drawn from them and the discussions we had during our time together. I owe thanks to Ian Borsuk, David Gifuni, Jamiey Kelly, Michaela Manson, Spiro Metaxas, Matthew Palynchuk, and Massimo Orsini. Special regard is owed to Alexander Agnello, who assisted by reading the entire manuscript.

Finally, I landed where I find myself at present. Utica College in New York has been tremendously supportive of this endeavor. Thomas Fryc, Robert Halliday, and Fred Zammiello have been integral in supporting me and allowing this project to come to completion.

Numerous audiences have also offered excellent comments on some of the ideas presented here. For their thoughtful insights, I would like to thank audiences at Concordia University, The University of Tübingen, Wilfred Laurier University and The University of Waterloo, The Canadian Disability Studies Association, Syracuse University School of Law, The University of Toronto, The University of California at Berkeley, The University of St.

Andrews, The World Congress of Rehabilitation International, and The Canadian Association for Health Services and Policy Research.

Many others have helped develop my thoughts, or provided guidance in many important ways throughout this project. Arash Farzam-Kia, Linnea Franits, Amanda Higgins, Brian Koslowski, Kayla Kwinter, Amanda Mcclenaghan, Adam Orfanakos, Luke Perry, Nelson Peters, Heather Rautiainen, Aaron Steacie, and Lidia de Tienda Palop: thank you.

I would especially like to thank Greg Affleck, Jeremy Butler, Frank Gairdner, Michael Kocsis, Mike Petrychanko, Doug Riddle, Mark Smith, and James Stuckey.

Joya Spina has been extremely encouraging and patient throughout this process and I am forever grateful for her kindness and love.

The most gratitude is owed to my parents however. My mother, Norma, continues to be unrelenting in her support of me and my endeavors, and my late father, Larry, was unwaveringly proud. It is to them that this book is dedicated.

I also wish to thank various coauthors, journals, and publishers for permission to draw on some previously published material in drafting some of the chapters of this book:

With kind permission from Springer Science + Business Media: Riddle, C. A. "Well-Being and the Capability of Health." *Topoi* 32, no. 2 (2013): 153–160.

With kind permission from Springer Science + Business Media: Riddle, C. A. "Defining Disability: Metaphysical Not Political." *Medicine, Health Care, & Philosophy* 16, no. 3 (2013): 377–384.

Riddle, C. A. "The Ontology of Impairment: Rethinking How We Define Disability." In *Emerging Perspectives on Disability Studies*, edited by Matthew Wappett and Katrina Arndt, 23–39. New York: Palgrave Macmillian, reproduced with permission of Palgrave Macmillan. The full published version of this publication is available at www.palgrave.com.

"Natural Diversity and Justice for People with Disabilities," by Christopher A. Riddle (from) *Disability and the Good Human Life*, edited by Jerome Bickenbach, Franziska Felder and Barbara Schmitz. Copyright © 2012 Cambridge University Press. Reprinted with permission.

Riddle, C. A. "Equality & Disability: A Charter Analysis." *Disability Stud-*

ies Quarterly 32, no. 1 (2012), reprinted by permission of the publisher (DSQ, http://dsq-sds.org).

By courtesy of LIT Verlag: Riddle, C. A. "Measuring Capabilities: The Case of Disability." In *The Capability Approach on Social Order*, edited by Niels Weidtmann, Yanti Martina Hölzchen, and Bilal Hawa (preface by Martha Nussbaum), 49–62. Munster: LIT Verlag, 2012.

Riddle, C. A. "Responsibility and Foundational Material Conditions." *The American Journal of Bioethics* 11, no. 7 (2011): 53–55, reprinted by permission of the publisher (Taylor & Francis Ltd, http://www.tandf.co.uk /journals).

Rioux M. H., and Riddle, C. A. "Values in Disability Policy & Law: Equality." In *Critical Perspectives On Human Rights and Disability Law*, edited by M. Rioux, L. Basser, and M. Jones, 37–55. The Hague: Brill/Martinus Nijhoff Publishers, 2011, reprinted by permission of the publisher (Brill, http://www.brill.com).

Riddle, C. A. "Indexing, Capabilities, and Disability." *The Journal of Social Philosophy* 41, no. 4 (2010): 527–537, reprinted with permission of the publisher (Wiley).

C.A.R.
Fall 2013

Chapter 1
Disability and Justice

"I guess the only time people think about injustice is when it happens to them."

Charles Bukowski, *Ham on Rye*

Surely it is not the case that most egalitarian theorists do not *care* about people with disabilities. Nonetheless, traditional views of justice have often theorized that people with disabilities and other marginalized individuals are beyond the scope of justice.[1] This is because, I think, many of the philosophers working on these problems are not disabled, and perhaps have not encountered a serious disability in their day-to-day lives in any meaningful way. Thus, perhaps an explanation for the exclusion of people with disabilities from the majority of contemporary egalitarian discourse is because those who are doing the theorizing have not experienced the kinds of injustice people with disabilities have, and consequently, have not been forced to think about it. This is not to suggest that in order to work on issues related to people with disabilities, one must be disabled themselves, but rather, it is something entirely different.[2] People with disabilities have been put by the wayside in a very innocent manner—most egalitarian theorists have often simply not thought about people with disabilities because, at first glance, the type of injustices they suffer do not closely resemble the type they are most familiar with or find most pressing.

In *Frontiers of Justice*, Martha Nussbaum makes disability a primary issue that we can no longer ignore. She argues that of the many problems

1

plaguing contemporary accounts of justice, there are three unsolved problems that deserve our utmost attention: impairment and disability; nationality; and species membership.[3] Nussbaum contends that disability, and particularly, its omission from the concerns of contemporary egalitarianism, is an especially pressing problem. Certainly the exclusion of people with disabilities from the domain within which judgments of justice are made is problematic for numerous reasons. First, by limiting the scope of justice to include only those who are *perceived* to have the ability to perform a particular act or function, classical theorists exclude a large segment of the population on the basis of ableist assumptions. In fact, the 2011 *World Report on Disability*, released by the World Health Organization, estimates that more than one billion people in the world (approximately 15 percent of our population) live with a disability and that nearly 200 million of these people experience difficulties in functioning.[4]

Second, while the injustices suffered by people with disabilities do not in any *immediately* obvious manner bear strong resemblances to the injustices suffered by able-bodied individuals, the consideration of people with disabilities within egalitarian conceptions of justice can serve to highlight general inadequacies with egalitarianism that do in fact, affect able-bodied persons. Problems of justice which affect able-bodied individuals are often in greater relief in people with disabilities, allowing for easier identification and rectification of unjust circumstances. Accordingly, the pursuit of justice for people with disabilities should no longer be viewed as an exploration soley for disability advocates or theorists, but should instead, be perceived as crucial to the advancement of egalitarian scholarship as a whole.

Theorists such as Rawls postpone the more extreme forms of need or deprivation that arise when examining disability. This is of course, most often by design and not omission. Nevertheless, no mechanism through which the inclusion of people with disabilities might take place is presented. This seems to run afoul of some of our most common intuitions regarding the purpose and goal of promoting a society of equals. The fair treatment of people with disabilities is surely difficult for classical theorists, because, as Nussbaum suggests, many people with disabilities require atypical social arrangements, including a wide variety of care.[5] Thus, if disabled individuals are to live integrated lives, they require recognition of the social barriers preventing their full participation—simply shifting the spotlight to individual deficiencies is inadequate.

With scarce resources and competing interests often pulling intuitions concerning the scope of justice in opposing directions, egalitarian theorists have arrived at an impasse. In what follows, I hope to initiate an escape from this predicament by highlighting some weaknesses of the capabilities approach in order for us to more closely approximate equality for people with disabilities.

As the subtitle of this book might suggest, I hope to inject a discussion of the practice of justice—of the applied aspects associated with the implementation of the capabilities approach in the context of disability. I do this not only because assuring justice for people with disabilities is of great interest to me, but also because I feel egalitarians have been theorizing in isolation.

Instead of acknowledging the primacy of disability, theorists have been striving toward justice in a misguided manner. We need to view the experience of disability as one that can lead our notion of equality to closer approximate justice. Instead, egalitarians, and more specifically, capability theorists, have been formulating a currency of egalitarian justice in the hopes that it can stand alone and bring people with disabilities along with it. In this sense, capability theorists have been putting the cart before the horse. They have been attempting to drag the disabled behind a conception of equality toward justice. Instead, they ought to be allowing the experiences of people with disabilities to lead equality to a just state of affairs. It is only when we properly affix the horse to the cart that we can begin to approximate justice for not only, but principally, people with disabilities.

Despite the postponement of questions of disability, theorists like Rawls drew our attention to the fact that people with disabilities are a paradigmatic example of the most marginalized and least advantaged within a pluralistic conception of well-being.

What follows is an attempt to address the questions concerning people with disabilities left by Rawls and other egalitarians or people concerned with distributive justice. Rawls's conception of justice as fairness is often viewed as a launching point for contemporary egalitarian theorizing,[6] and it is my belief that in order to promote an adequate and inclusive notion of justice, the accommodation of people with disabilities into egalitarian thought must be accomplished. I suggest that the capabilities approach can retain Rawls's notion that principles of equality should be designed to regulate the kinds of social cooperation to be promoted,[7] while moving beyond the narrow answer to the question of who should be included within the scope of equality.

Without a proper account of the currency of egalitarian justice, many of our political and moral intuitions become answers to large philosophical questions with little practical significance.[8]

Equality is entrenched in the constitutions of some countries and is accepted in many others as fundamental to the notion of governance. It often assumes that certain basic problems are likely to occur and seeks to address the way in which rules are fashioned and how institutions, rights, and duties are organized and defended. The notion of equality has been used as an organizing framework, at least nominally, without having a foundational framework established that is inclusive of all those we wish to promote justice for.

The impasse that has emerged within contemporary egalitarian discourse threatens both theoretical and empirical development in political philosophy and society. What follows is an attempt to offer critical insight into the capabilities approach and how the injustices currently perpetuated against people with disabilities are largely left unaddressed by such an understanding of justice.

As a helpful guide, one might view this work as divided into two broad categories.

The Conceptual

Chapters 2 and 3 both serve as conceptual primers for the contextualized criticisms that follow.

Chapter 2, "Defining Disability," examines what we mean when we classify or diagnose someone as being disabled. This question is asked for at least two reasons. First, it helps us to better understand why contemporary egalitarian theories have failed to provide an adequate minimal conception of justice for the disabled. Second, it ensures we all have a relatively similar understanding of what is at stake. It ensures we are referring to the same group of people when we make the claim that a theory of justice appears to be inadequate because it excludes people with disabilities in the manners discussed in chapters 4, 5, and 6.

Justice theorists have failed to promote an adequate conception of justice for people with disabilities because first, people with disabilities have often been excluded from the scope of justice altogether. For example, Robert Nozick acknowledged that people were disabilities were "disadvantaged," but suggested that these forms of disadvantage were to be addressed outside the realm of justice, through charity or acts of benevolence.[9]

Second, theorists have also been working with an inadequate conception of disability—this is why it is important we specify precisely what we mean when we state that someone is a person with a disability, or that some condition results in a disability. For example, Mark Stein classified disability as a health related condition—as disability, pain, and injury.[10]

If we adopt a conception of justice that relies upon an insufficient understanding of what constitutes "disability," it is no wonder existing conceptions of egalitarianism are unable to promote the full inclusion of people with disabilities.

I, like Nussbaum before me, take for granted that first, the accommodation of people with disabilities is within the scope of justice. If we are attempting to establish an adequate minimal conception of justice, the inclusion of people with disabilities within the realm of those to whom justice is owed is essential. Second, I suggest that disability is a complex relationship between traits inherent to an individual, and the socially created, external barriers to that individual.[11] This later claim is perhaps more contentious and is certainly more difficult to establish.

The difficulty in establishing this claim is evidenced by the fact that recent discussions surrounding the conceptualizing of disability have resulted in a stalemate between British sociologists and philosophers. The stagnation of theorizing that has occurred threatens not only academic pursuits and the advancement of theoretical interpretations within the Disability Studies community, but also how we educate and advocate politically, legally, and socially.

More pointedly, many activists and theorists in the UK appear to believe the British social model is the only effective means of understanding and advocating on behalf of people with disabilities.[12] This model, largely reliant upon materialist research traditions, contends that disability is a form of social oppression and hence, is a phenomenon that should be conceptualized in social terms.[13] Individual properties such as impairments tend to be disregarded or minimized as they are viewed to be unimportant in the analysis of the social causes of disability.

Concurrently, many bioethicists and philosophers have embraced what Tom Shakespeare has classified as an "Interactional Approach" to disability—that "the experience of a disabled person results from the relationship between factors intrinsic to the individual, and the extrinsic factors arising from the wider context in which she finds herself."[14]

The arguments advanced in chapter 2 are set out to demonstrate that the benefits of the British social model are now outweighed by its burdens. I suggest, as Jerome Bickenbach has, that while it may be somewhat churlish to critique the social model in light of its political success, taken literally, it implies that people with disabilities require no additional health resources by virtue of their impairments.[15]

Despite the eloquent arguments that have preceded me by interactional theorists,[16] very few have been accepted as evidence of fallacious reasoning by British social model theorists. The second chapter is an attempt to clarify why it is that the types of arguments British social model theorists have been offering are misguided. I suggest that the British social model, unlike an interactional approach, is unable to provide a realistic account of the experience of disability, and subsequently, unable to be properly utilized to ensure justice for people with disabilities.

Chapter 3, "The Capabilities Approach," also provides a conceptual analysis. It begins by providing a thorough background of the capabilities approach. I highlight the difference between capabilities (substantial freedoms—what a person is able to be or do) and functionings (active realizations of a capability or set of capabilities), and stress Nussbaum's emphasis on the former, rather than the latter.

Next, I briefly justify what might at first glance be thought to be a hasty move to the capability approach. I appeal to Amartya Sen's critical analysis given in his Tanner Lecture and also briefly examine the more recent work of Mark Stein prior to moving to a critical engagement with the capabilities approach.

I endorse Sen's critical engagement with welfarism, and suggest that strict welfare-based conceptions of justice are inadequate. I, like Sen, believe that welfare-based conceptions of justice compound, rather than rectify, injustices against people with disabilities.

I move on to address why Sen deemed it necessary to push away from a resource-based conception of justice, and in particular, a Rawlsian conception of resources. I suggest that despite it being a somewhat dated critical appraisal of resourcism, that Sen's critical engagement is still relevant today.[17]

And while capability theory does not go without criticism in contemporary literature, I feel there is a great deal of room for the kind of critiques that might be established when taking people with disabilities into consideration. I offer three interrelated critiques against the capabilities approach in an attempt to gain insight into the changes necessary to adequately promote justice for people with disabilities.

In Practice

Chapters 4, 5, and 6 all engage in a critical examination of the capabilities approach by taking into account the experience of disability and the difficulties that may arise in the promotion of justice as a result of that experience.

The first critique I launch involves a distinction I make between horizontal spectral analysis (the ordering of a capability among other capabilities) and vertical spectral analysis (the assessment of the opportunity or ability to achieve, secure, or perform a particular capability distinct from considerations of the relationship to other capabilities).

Chapter 4, "The Indexing Problem," begins to make this distinction by focusing on an analogy put forth by Wolff and De-Shalit. In *Disadvantage*, they acknowledge the necessity of ranking the various capabilities and employ a mechanism they refer to as "complex evaluation" to provide a more robust classification of well-being. They cite decathlon scoring as a prime example of how to weigh seemingly different events to arrive at a singular conclusion about an individual's overall performance. In the case of a decathlon, the performance being evaluated is an individual's athletic ability. In the case of capabilities, the evaluation is being made about an individual's well-being.

I follow Wolff and De-Shalit's discussion concerning the decathlon analogy and concur with their conclusion that first, we can, in theory, measure well-being through a complex system of evaluation. Second, I agree with their astute point that we must arrive at at least a partial ranking of capabilities. Here Wolff and De-Shalit offer what I think is a compelling example shoring up this claim.

I then utilize this decathlon analogy to develop the distinction between horizontal spectral analysis and vertical spectral analysis that I mentioned briefly above. I believe that this analogy can also shed light on what I view to be a more serious problem plaguing the capabilities approach. Recall, I refer to the ordering of capabilities as the horizontal spectral analysis–the ranking of capabilities among other capabilities. Wolff and De-Shalit acknowledge, at least in part, that a horizontal spectral analysis must occur in order to arrive at a minimally just notion of well-being within a capabilities perspective.

The primary claim made by me in this chapter, however, involves the measurement of particular functionings. I believe the decathlon analogy can also assist us in examining this aspect of capability theory. I call this assessment the vertical spectral analysis—the assessment of the opportunity or ability to achieve, secure, or perform a particular capability, distinct from considerations of the relationship to other capabilities. An adequate account of particular capabilities requires factoring in the social variations that impede our ability to properly situate individuals above or below a fundamental threshold.

Chapter 4 advances an argument that suggests the capabilities approach is unable to properly take these social variations into account, and as such, fails to adequately perform a vertical spectral analysis. I argue that our inability to properly complete this analysis is one of the three primary problems associated with the capabilities approach.

After exploring the inability of the capabilities approach to properly assess need, I begin to explore the further subtleties associated with how conceptions of justice identify and rectify the situations of the less well-off. Chapter 5, "Stigma-Sensitivity," takes a closer look at critiques launched by Thomas Pogge against Nussbaum, as well as the response given from Elizabeth Anderson in support of the capabilities approach.

Pogge suggests that the capabilities approach stigmatizes individuals in both the assessment of need and provision of resources and accommodation, thus undermining an essential aspect of one's human dignity. Here I ignore, if only briefly, the claims I made previously about the inability of the capabilities approach to adequately assess need, and instead, examine how it would go about performing that function were it able to complete a vertical spectral analysis. In other words, I ask, if the capability approach were able to assess need, would it stigmatize individuals in the process?

Chapter 5 advances an argument that suggests that one of the primary measures of the success or failure of a conception of egalitarian justice ought to be its ability to avoid the further stigmatization of vulnerable populations. I refer to the ability to not further stigmatize individuals on the basis of naturally acquired skills or endowments as "stigma-sensitivity." With reference to the above question, I argue that despite the clear strengths of the capabilities approach, it nevertheless fails to be as stigma-sensitive as alternative conceptions. I suggest that it does in fact, unnecessarily potentially stigmatize individuals further on the basis of naturally acquired skills or endowments.

Here Pogge offers both an explicit, and implicit critique of the capabilities approach that I believe Elizabeth Anderson and I successfully shield the approach from. However, I suggest that the capabilities approach is, by its very design, prone to being less stigma-sensitive than numerous other conceptualizations of justice.

More specifically, I suggest that when examining competing claims of justice, attention ought to be paid to how we might begin to operationalize redistributive measures and assess need in a society where these values of equality and justice are endorsed. I make a modest and, I think, self-evident claim that, when comparing two equally desirable conceptions of justice, priority ought to be given to the conceptualization that is more stigma-sensitive—that stigmatizes those in need less than other, competing claims. I then go on to defend a more ambitious claim, suggesting that strict opportunity-based accounts of distributive justice increase the likelihood of further marginalizing individuals on the basis of naturally acquired skills or endowments.

Chapter 6, "The Special Moral Importance of Health" places an emphasis on health. It picks up the question concerning the desirability (perhaps even the necessity) of performing a horizontal spectral analysis that was put aside in chapter 4. I assert, as Norman Daniels has before me, that a conception of justice must acknowledge the special moral importance of health. I proceed by first, outlining the manner in which Daniels defends the claim that health has special moral importance. Second, I use this examination as a launching point to examine how the capabilities approach can address the topics of justice and health.

I argue that a focus on disadvantage can begin to satisfactorily explain why health ought to receive special moral importance. I suggest a more nuanced recognition of Sen's notion of "basic capabilities" can get us closer to adequately characterizing capabilities.

I do this by first presenting a scenario involving two individuals, both of whom lack access to only one capability. The first cannot secure the capability of bodily health due to an unhealthy lifestyle, whilst the second lacks access to bodily integrity due to a life of celibacy. Second, I explore these scenarios by assessing the nature of disadvantage suffered in both instances. I suggest that corrosive disadvantage (or the type of disadvantage that adversely impacts one's ability to secure other valuable things) is what leads us to conclude that health is of special moral importance in the promotion of justice and the endorsing of well-being.

Concluding Remarks

Chapters 2 and 3 lay the groundwork for the criticisms launched against the capabilities approach in chapters 4, 5, and 6. I offer critical remarks against the capabilities approach, not because I feel it is a weak conception of justice, but because I feel it is the strongest offering at present. The criticisms I launch were crafted with an eye on strengthening the capabilities approach, and not to offer disparaging remarks against those working in the area. I sincerely hope that the criticisms advanced in this text can serve to allow the capabilities approach to more closely approximate justice for people with disabilities. Precisely how we go about doing this is not for me to say.

Notes

1. John Rawls, *Political Liberalism* (New York: Columbia University Press, 1993); Bernard Williams, "The Idea of Equality," in *Philosophy, Politics, and Society (Second Series)*, ed. Peter Laslett and W. G. Runciman (Oxford: Oxford University Press, 1969), 110–31.

2. For an excellent discussion about this matter, see Simo Vehmas, *Deviance, Difference and Human Variety: The Moral Significance of Disability in Modern Bioethics* (Turku: Turun Yliopisto, 2002), 20–24.

3. Martha Nussbaum, *Frontiers of Justice: Disability, Nationality and Species Membership* (Cambridge: The Belknap Press of Harvard University Press, 2006), 14.

4. World Health Organization, *World Report on Disability* (Geneva: World Health Organization, 2011), xi

5. Nussbaum, *Frontiers of Justice*, 99.

6. Nussbaum, *Frontiers of Justice*, 99.

7. John Rawls, *A Theory of Justice* (Cambridge: Harvard University Press, 1971), 11.

8. Nussbaum, *Frontiers of Justice*, 415.

9. Robert Nozick, *Anarchy, State & Utopia* (New York: Basic Books, 1974).

10. Mark Stein, *Distributive Justice and Disability: Utilitarianism Against Egalitarianism* (New Haven: Yale University Press, 2006), 24.

11. Tom Shakespeare, *Disability Rights and Wrongs* (New York: Routledge, 2006).

12. Shakespeare, *Disability Rights and Wrongs*.

13. Simo Vehmas and Pekka Makela, "A Realist Account of the Ontology of Impairment," *Journal of Medical Ethics* 34, no. 2 (2008): 93–95.

14. Shakespeare, *Rights and Wrongs*, 55.

15. Jerome E. Bickenbach, "Measuring Health: The Disability Critique Revisited," paper presented at the *Third Annual International Conference on Ethical issues in the Measurement of Health and the Global Burden of Disease* (Cambridge, Massachusetts: Harvard University School of Public Health, April 24–25 2008).

16. Examples of these arguments will be provided in chapter 2. That said, perhaps most noteworthy of these critiques are the following: Shakespeare, *Rights and Wrongs*; Simo Vehmas and Pekka Makela, "The Ontology of Disability & Impairment: A Discussion of the Natural and Social Features," in *Arguing about Disability: Philosophical Perspectives*, ed. K. Kristiansen, S. Vehmas, and T. Shakespeare (London: Routledge, 2008); Jerome Bickenbach et al., "Models of Disablement, Universalism, and the International Classification of Impairments, Disabilities and Handicaps," *Social Science and Medicine* 48, no. 1 (1999): 1173–87; and World Health Organization, *International Classification of Functioning, Disability and Health* (Geneva: World Health Organization, 2001).

17. The sharp distinction between welfare-based conceptions of justice and resource-based conceptions of justice was perhaps best made by Ronald Dworkin. Dworkin offers a thorough rebuttal of welfarism prior to moving to defend his conception of a resource-based conception of justice in Ronald Dworkin, "What is Equality? Part 1: Equality of Welfare." *Philosophy and Public Affairs* 10, no. 3 (1981): 185–236; and Ronald Dworkin, "What is

Equality? Part 2: Equality of Resources." *Philosophy and Public Affairs* 10, no. 4 (1981): 283–345; and later in Ronald Dworkin, *Sovereign Virtue: The Theory and Practice of Equality* (Cambridge: Harvard University Press, 2000).

Chapter 2
Defining Disability

As mentioned previously, recent discussions surrounding the conceptualizing of disability have resulted in a stalemate between British sociologists and philosophers. While many activists and theorists in the UK argue that the British "social model" is the only effective means of understanding and advocating on behalf of people with disabilities,[1] many bioethicists and philosophers have embraced an "interactional approach" to disability.

The impasse at which we find ourselves is threatening our ability to successfully accommodate people with disabilities within our conceptions of morality and justice. We must move beyond the disputes focusing on the nature of disability and instead, shift our focus to what we can do for people with disabilities by using the best conception of disability available to us. In what follows, I aim to articulate why we ought to be endorsing an interactional approach to disability. Ultimately, the understanding of disability that is being employed is a *working definition* and that in the obvious absence of universal agreement; some people are bound to disagree with the conception being endorsed. Nonetheless, I hope that should one find themselves in disagreement with what follows in this chapter, that one will suspend potential criticisms for the sake of advancing a meaningful discussion about disability and justice—a discussion that could not occur without some working definition of disability.

I will begin by outlining precisely what is at stake here—what each of the three so-called models represent. Secondly, I will introduce some general remarks in favor of the interactional model. I will then restate and extend the critique that I view to be one of the most convincing and thorough refutations of the social model of disability. I will conclude by characterizing the nature of this debate in a new light to demonstrate why the criticisms from British social model theorists ought not to be taken seriously. More pointedly, I intend to restate and advance existing critiques of the social model of disability and to also present this debate in a novel manner to demonstrate why social model theorists have offered, in my mind, no significant criticisms of the interactional model of disability.

I do all of the above with an eye on clarifying what it is that we mean when we talk about disability to ensure we have a solid foundation to work from when attempting to operationalize the capabilities approach in subsequent chapters.

What are the "Models" of Disability?

First, it might prove helpful to begin by clarifying precisely what it is that one is referring to when using the phrases "social model," "British social model," or any other immediately obviously variants used interchangeably. The understanding of disability that emerges from such a model can I think, rightly be seen as originating from a push away from medicalized understandings (or "medical model" ways of thinking) of what it means when we talk about disability. More specifically, social model theorists reject the idea that we can define disability as some sort of medically observable deviation from biomedical norms. These deviations from the norm can, according to medical model theorists, be attributed to disease, trauma, or other health-related conditions.[2] We can hash out these differences between the social model and the medical model further by examining what it is that each model would endorse by way of intervention to undo any hardships resulting from disability.

The medical model, of course, treats any functional limitations that arise from the experience of disability as a medical phenomenon, treatable by medical or technological means and perhaps even preventable through biological engineering or screening. This model is also sometimes referred to as an individual pathological model due to its focus on the inability of individuals.[3]

Conversely, the social model adopts a social pathological approach and sees preventative measures associated with the ill effects of disability as originating in the elimination of social, attitudinal, geographical, political, and legal barriers. A social model theorist views the disabling effects associated with the experience of disability as resulting from social organization, and not as residing in individuals. Michael Oliver offers what I view to be a paradigmatic quote to summarize this position. He states, "it is not individual limitations, of whatever kind, which are the cause of the problem, but society's failure to provide appropriate services and adequately ensure the needs of disabled people are fully taken into account in its social organization."[4]

To clarify matters further, we can focus on a distinction typically made by social model theorists. The social model makes a distinction between impairment and disability, suggesting that while impairment can be defined in individual and biological terms, disability instead ought to be defined as a social creation.[5] According to social model theorists, disability is what makes impairment a problem. The guiding belief here is that the social barriers and oppression resulting from these barriers are what constitute disability. In other words, impairment is not a problem, it is the way difference and impairment manifest themselves in our social institutions that results in a problem.[6] Social model theorists have tended to rely upon this dichotomous way of characterizing debates associated with the definition of disability. This strict binary is one that no longer exists in any important way.

Interactional model theorists instead believe that we require a different understanding of disability than what this rigid dichotomy can offer us. Instead, disability ought to be regarded as a complex interaction between the traits inherent to a person (or one's impairment), and how these traits manifest themselves in the environment they find themselves in (the disabling facts of one's impairment). Shakespeare sums up this position eloquently when he says "there can be no impairment without society, nor disability without impairment."[7] After all, without having an impairment, if we rely upon the characterization of impairment given to us by social model theorists, it is impossible to experience disabling barriers.

Shakespeare states, and I think rightly, that while impairments may not be a sufficient cause of the hardships or difficulties people with disabilities must endure, impairments appear to be necessary.[8] If there is no relationship of this sort between impairment and disability, then disability becomes a vacuous, all-encompassing term, including any and all forms of social oppression.[9] The thought here is that "even in the most accessible world, there will always be residual disadvantage attached to many impairments."[10]

It is important to note that there is causality present between impairment and disability for interactional theorists that is not necessarily relevant for the examination being done by social model theorists. I will reexamine this topic in greater depth later when I introduce the work of Simo Vehmas, who I think provides an outstanding argument, and indeed perhaps the best critical remarks to date, against social model theorists.

Putting this issue aside temporarily, the so-called interactional model has been presented in various forms previously. The interactional model has appeared both as philosophical arguments, such as those examined in this chapter, made by Shakespeare, Vehmas, and Bickenbach, as well as policies or classificatory instruments (the 1980 *International Classification of Im-*

pairments, Disability, and Handicaps [ICIDH] and the 2001 *International Classification of Functioning, Disability and Health* [ICF]).

There is an interesting relationship between the establishment of sound philosophical principles and the introduction of public policy, with most of those involved in the latter also typically involved in the former. This observation leads us to conclude that the philosophical positions were designed to inform our social policy, and that these social policies or classificatory instruments were designed to adequately characterize disability to begin to redress some of the injustices currently perpetuated against people with disabilities.

What Did the Social Model Offer?

I hope the preceding discussion was an adequate cursory glance at what understandings of disability are at odds. That said, I think it is of importance to mention some redeemable features of the social model prior to introducing some critical remarks. The social model has undeniably had tremendous political success. It has, in some rather obvious ways, increased the well-being of people with disabilities globally. The introduction of the social model was said to result in a paradigm shift in the manner in which disability was viewed.[11]

The introduction of this model was also said to not only have an influence on welfare provision and professional practice, but on the consciousness of disabled people as well.[12] To many, this model appears to be the linchpin upon which contemporary disability rights challenges rely.[13] This model first solidified a fractured movement by identifying a central political strategy: the removal of social barriers.[14] If we conceptualized the difficulties encountered by people with disabilities as resulting from discrimination, then we could begin to take active political measures to avoid or rectify discriminatory practices. We saw the actions of the disability movement influence anti-discrimination legislation focused on human rights violations, modeled after the Americans with Disabilities Act and the British Equal Opportunities and Race Relations laws.[15]

Second, as mentioned in passing previously, this model liberated many people with disabilities. People were able to deflect blame for an inability to achieve an end from themselves to social structures that disabled. People with disabilities became empowered, and no longer did they have to feel sorry for themselves for being defective—they did not have to change: society had to.[16] Instead of feeling at fault, people with disabilities could feel angry. They could feel angry that society was structured in such a manner that they were limited in ways others were not.

What's Wrong with the Social Model?

All that said, while being a useful political tool, the social model of disability does not reflect what is actually experienced by people with disabilities. If we are after a model to characterize the reality of the experience of disability, the social model is not it. In what follows, I focus on three interrelated critiques of the social model of disability. I classify these critiques as: i) medical (those concerning the treatment of individual impairments); ii) social (those concerning the interconnectedness and causality of impairment and disability); and iii) ontological (those concerned with assessing the metaphysical basis of the experience of disability).

Medical Critiques

For a paradigmatic example of a medical critique of the social model of disability, let us look to a passing remark offered by Bickenbach that I previously made mention of.[17] Bickenbach stated that, taken literally, the social model implies that no interventions are necessary to provide health resources to those with disabilities. He concluded that this was, I think rather obviously, unjust and undignified.[18]

Take for example, an individual who experiences both functional limitations associated with movement as well as pain associated with that movement.[19] We do not have to stress our imaginations much at all to arrive at a nonfanciful example: arthritic pain. When suffering from advanced stages of arthritis, one's ability to function or move is impaired, in additional to one experiencing a great deal of pain when attempting to perform those functions. The social model, taken literally, recommends altering social arrangements to reduce the extent to which such an individual is required to, for example, involve intricate movements of his or her hands in day-to-day activities. It says nothing about required medical interventions or the reallocation of special health resources associated with the amelioration of that pain. Recall, the social model fails to acknowledge the importance of the causal relationship between impairment and disability. In other words, in this example, the social model does little to rectify the experience of pain (or welfare deficiencies), while tending only to functional limitations (or resource deficiencies).[20]

That said, the endorsements made by social model theorists may do something to reduce pain. After all, if one is required to perform less intricate movements with one's hands, surely the extent to which that individual experiences pain would be minimized. However, considering the potential medical interventions at our disposal, is the mere minimization of pain not inadequate? Would we not be promoting a greater form of well-being if we tended to this welfare deficiency? Would we not be unjust in permitting this kind of avoidable suffering when an individual or medical intervention would almost surely reduce it to a much greater extent (or perhaps even entirely)?

I posit that it would be unreasonable to reject one's claim to medical interventions to reduce this sort of pain by denying the importance of the causal relationship between impairment and disability. To refuse to take individual initiatives to reduce pain through individual medical interventions is a serious injustice in this instance. We have an obligation to intervene to provide health care and resources—an obligation a social model theorist, strictly speaking, cannot account for.

Social Critiques

I think Shakespeare provides us with an excellent example of a social critique. These criticisms focus on the causal relationship between impairment and disability. They tend to reinforce the interconnectedness of impairment to social oppression, while acknowledging the importance of impairment that social model proponents reject.

Shakespeare suggests that to make a distinction between impairment and disability, and to suggest that the latter is social and the former not, is incorrect.[21] He argues that "what counts as impairment is a social judgement."[22] After all, it is primarily the values within a particular culture that determine what an impairment is. Perhaps less importantly, attitudes of the wider society impact how many people with impairments there are.[23]

Shakespeare points us to the fact that the "visibility and salience of impairment depend on the expectations and arrangements in a particular society."[24] He uses dyslexia as an example to further highlight his point: dyslexia may not be a problem for an individual until society places a demand on its citizens to be literate.[25]

This example shows quite clearly I think, that impairment is, at least partially, social—that how we conceptualize impairment can be a cultural issue.[26] Impairment is not of course, presocial. It is only ever viewed through social relations.

This shows an "inextricable interconnection [between] impairment and disability."[27] More pointedly, it demonstrates that both impairment and disability must be taken into consideration when theorizing about justice and disability.

Perhaps more importantly, this example demonstrates that these different factors (both social and personal) are not only inextricably linked, but that they compound each other through a complex relationship of how the traits inherent to the individual manifest themselves socially.[28] In other words, impairment has both physical and social dimensions and to deny the importance of the causal relationship between impairment and disability is to ignore an important component associated with the experience of disability.

Ontological Critiques

Finally, let us look to an example of an ontological critique of the social model of disability. I suspect that critiques of this nature tend to be the most damning of the three explored in this chapter.

I think Simo Vehmas has perhaps most convincingly argued against social model theorists. His argument against the social model is incredibly strong and has received little by way of response from social model theorists.

Vehmas responded to criticisms against Shakespeare that appeared in a symposium in the journal *Disability & Society*. Here he argues that we must make a distinction between the subjective and the objective in the ontology of disability. He claims that "in the ontological sense, objective and subjective are predicates of the entities in the world."[29] Objective entities, in the ontological sense, are existent independent of any perceiver.[30] Conversely, if Vehmas is correct, things such as pains are subjective insofar as they are dependent upon a perceiver being present to experience them.

Vehmas invokes the imagery of a mountain and claims that mountains are ontologically objective because if we ceased to exist, or if there was nothing perceiving a mountain, it would nevertheless continue to exist—a mountain's mode of existence is independent of perception. Individuals with Trisomy 21 (or the chromosomal disorder caused by the presence of an extra twenty-first chromosome) are not inherently predisposed to oppression—the extra twenty-first chromosome exists independently, regardless of how we feel about its presence. The presence of an additional chromosome does, however, include what Vehmas refers to as "observer-relative features"[31] as well. These observer-related features do not add any material objects to reality, but they do, according to Vehmas, add epistemically objective features where the features exist relative to human beings.

Thus, Down syndrome is caused by the chromosomal disorder involving an extra twenty-first chromosome: Trisomy 21. This is a fact or truth that exists independently of what sort of views we hold. Here Vehmas invokes the language of Searle to make a distinction between *brute facts* and *institu-*

tional facts.[32] Before we can agree on any particular institutional facts, we must of course, have brute facts. We can see why this is necessarily so by examining any of the human institutions we interact with every day. In order for there to be money, games, schools, or any other human institution, there must be a physical realization of that institution.[33] In order for there to be "school" there must exist the physical, brick and mortar object, where I was writing this. More generally, Vehmas claims there must be "some brute fact on which we can impose [a] social function."[34]

This observation exposes the devastatingly untenable position of social model theorists. As mentioned above, according to these theorists, disability is a socially derived phenomenon, resulting from oppression against people. Vehmas highlights the fact that, "[by] definition [. . .] disability as a social phenomenon includes not just a mere institutional level, but a brute level of facts as well, namely, impairments."[35] Thus, social model theorists are only acknowledging part of the phenomenon of disability. For Vehmas, the problem with social model conceptualizations of disability is that their "foundation[s] [are] based on the upper stairs of the ontological ladder, as it were, and that [they] [ignore] the inevitable physical foundation of the social phenonmena."[36]

Vehmas has acknowledged elsewhere that "[i]f the unfortunateness of some condition actually results from communal values and social arrangements, that particular condition is a *contingent* disability—it has been determined and created by accidental and arbitrary factors."[37] This minor concession on Vehmas's part exposes one further point to be made.

As important as Vehmas's claim is, it is important to note the converse as well: that impairment, while not always, can be bad in and of itself. In other words, disabilities are not *always* contingent. Impairments can have devastating effects on individuals, even with no social arrangements compounding those ill effects. Certainly social circumstances can exacerbate or minimize the effects of impairment, but oftentimes, even in the complete absence of the effects of social arrangements, impairments can negatively impact well-being. John Harris has suggested that impairments must necessarily have negative impacts for individuals, otherwise, we do not consider the social oppression resulting from the condition as a disability at all.[38]

To highlight this point, let us return to an example presented earlier. If we revisit the example of the individual with arthritis, we can see that impairment plays an important role in defining and addressing disability. Even if we placed no demanding requirements upon individuals with arthritis to use their hands to complete intricate or repetitive movements—if we did all we could to mitigate the ill effects imposed onto these individuals' impairments by society—they would nonetheless suffer pain. If we remove all socially derived disadvantage from the equation, impairment remains, as do the ill effects associated with it. Even if we remove all the disabling social, legal, environmental, and attitudinal barriers that lead to contingent disabilities, in some instances such as the example above, impairment remains, and is potentially devastatingly problematic.[39] This modest point reinforces the causal relationship between impairment and disability, and shores up the beliefs that impairment must be taken seriously within disability studies, for it can have damaging effects in and of itself.

Why Have Social Model Theorists Failed to Engage in the Debate?

That all said, I think the best way of characterizing the debate thus far is as follows. I believe that social model theorists have entered a debate that they have failed to engage in. This failure to engage is, I think, a very innocent failure. This is to say, I do not suspect they are aware that they have entered a debate with a different mandate than their own. The criticisms most often launched against interactional theorists tend to revolve around what might happen to people with disabilities if the interactionalist position were true. Or perhaps more succinctly, they are concerned with how people with disabilities might be perceived, and how this, in turn, might affect social policy, legal decisions, the built environment, and more obviously, attitudinal barriers. They are concerned that the political success the social model has had will unravel and society will regress into the old, medical model ways of viewing people with disabilities. This would understandably, have tremendously negative impacts on the lives of the disabled. While this would in fact have negative impacts on people with disabilities, this should call our attention to formulating our public policies and our conceptual notions such as justice and morality more carefully and not to shifting our definition of disability to one that is inaccurate, but more convenient. To use Vehmas's words, "the horse before the disability studies carriage is often politics, not science"[40]—this should not be the case.

Take for example Michael Oliver. He has argued that the interactionalist position has "diminish[ed] [social model theorists'] past achievements."[41] He discusses numerous "realities of severe impairment"[42] that Shakespeare has ignored in advocating on behalf of an interactional model. What is implied here is quite vast, but I think the most obvious concern permeating this point is that by allowing a redirection of attention back toward impairment, we risk shifting back to medicalized ways of viewing disability, and consequently, risk reenacting the troubling treatment of people with disabilities of the past. He says quite explicitly that by Shakespeare endorsing an interactional approach, he is "making dangerous comments about social and legal change."[43] Here Oliver is suggesting that we ought to be concerned about the political and legal implications associated with how we define disability.

For another example, let us look at the remarks made by Marcia Rioux in the *Journal of Intellectual Disability Research*. She suggests that if we, when answering questions about disability, attempt to rely on "a world of 'disability facts,'"[44] we become unconscious about the judgments we make in doing so. In other words, in defining disability, we have to keep in mind the political implications for, and the judgments we make about, people with disabilities in the process. She claims, "[t]he judgments we make about the causes of disability, about the meaning of the concept and about the factors to hold responsible for the experience of disability have profound consequences for the directions pursued by advocates, policy-makers, politicians and the courts."[45]

More pointedly still, Rioux thinks that what is important in our defining of disability is that in that definition, we direct those she mentions (advocates, policy-makers, politicians, and the courts) toward the pursuit of what is perceived by her and other social model theorists to be the correct political mandate.

These concerns about social and legal change are not of *direct* interest to interactional theorists however. This is not to say interactional theorists are not concerned with enacting real, positive change, but rather, to simply suggest that they realize there is an ontological question to be tackled prior to enacting this change.

Take the following example to highlight the point I am attempting to make. Let us ask the question: "Who or what is Santa Claus?." We can answer this question differently when attempting to achieve different goals. Let us imagine there are only two potential mandates we might have when answering this question.

The first mandate is to promote the happiness of children and to enjoy a festive season. Most children in Western societies, barring religious observances that prevent a belief in Santa Claus, will be told that Santa Claus does in fact exist, and that he delivers presents to well-behaved children on the evening of December 24th while they sleep. He flies in a sled led by reindeer and enters homes through their chimneys by touching his nose to raise and lower himself. He then places toys, candies, and other goodies in stockings hung on a mantel and under an evergreen tree that had previously been decorated by parents and children in a ceremonious fashion. Among many other reasons, I'm sure, parents tell their children this occurs when asked about Santa Claus because other children will be told this, and perhaps they have been told this, and they have fond memories from their childhood, and they wish their children to have similar memories.

I think it is safe to say that the parents that choose to tell their children of the existence of Santa Claus do not believe Santa Claus actually exists. Nonetheless, what these parents actually believe about Santa Claus metaphysically is largely irrelevant. One might even say that they are not concerned about whether Santa Claus exists when they answer this question. They are not concerned with the reality of Santa. Their concern is about the immediate practical implications of them telling their children tales of Santa. They are concerned with how those around them will react to this "knowledge."

Next, let us imagine that we are air traffic controllers, we are scheduled to work the evening of December 24th, and we have received an anonymous tip that an entity referred to as "Santa Claus" is planning to fly through our airspace that evening. Thus, our mandate is not to ensure the happiness of our children during a festive season, but rather, when attempting to answer the question, "who or what is Santa Claus?," we are asking a question about the ontology of Santa Claus. We are asking what this thing is, and if we need to take it into account in performing our duties that evening. Our question is not "how do I make my children happy this Christmas?," but instead, "how do I regulate air traffic on the evening of the 24th?," or perhaps more specifically still, "what *things* do I have to take into account in performing my job, and is this *thing* one of them?."

Unlike the parents who have little concern about what Santa actually is, the question we are asking about Santa is more related to the metaphysics of Santa Claus. We want to know what, if in regulating air traffic, kind of things we have to take into account. We want to know what it is we ought to expect in terms of flying entities, and if Santa Claus might be a concern for us that evening. We go about answering this question by establishing first, who or what Santa Claus is. This is because of course, many entities will be in our airspace that evening. Birds, airplanes, precipitation, and insects are among the things we concern ourselves with in performing our duties. Surely not all of these things are of importance, however. What we do to determine if we ought to take a particular thing into account in performing our duties is ask questions about the ontology of that thing.

We explore what an "insect" is, and after we have answered metaphysical questions about insects, we can determine we need not, in most scenarios, take them into account in regulating air traffic. In a similar manner, when we are tipped off about the mysterious entity of "Santa Claus" entering our airspace, we ask questions about the ontology of this entity to determine if it ought to be taken into our calculations. Parents ask no such questions about Santa Claus in advancing their mandate.

It would be wrong to say that we as air traffic controllers are not concerned about the implications of the assertion that Santa does or does not exist. However, we are concerned about a proper characterization of Santa Claus first. We are aiming at articulating precisely who or what Santa is, and only then, assessing how this being figures into greater problems. We are putting aside the potentially uncomfortable implications involved with uncovering the reality of who or what Santa Claus is (i.e., children losing faith and becoming unhappy), in an attempt to uncover the truth first and foremost. In short, we are concerned about the ontology of Santa.

Irrespective of what the parents actually believe about the ontology of Santa, I think it should be immediately obvious that for them to suggest the air traffic controllers' conceptualization of Santa is wrong because it did not factor in the well-being of the children explicitly would be incorrect. The two are in fact, engaged in advancing entirely different mandates. In this instance, the parents seem to be suggesting that the proper conception of something is the one that leads to the best outcome, irrespective of how that conception corresponds with reality. To suggest that we as air traffic controllers have been getting it wrong is to not respond to arguments in kind. This is, rather obviously I think, entering a debate with air traffic controllers about the nature of Santa, while failing to engage in it.

Similarly, social model theorists have tended to assert that the proper conception of disability must be the one that corresponds most closely to an interpretation of the experience of disability that promotes the greatest form of well-being. But an account of disability does not, and should not, factor in political or social factors such as those social model theorists seem to think ought to be taken into account. It is important to mention that the political and social factors mentioned above that ought not to be taken into account are not the political and sociological factors that lead one's impairment to result in disabling barriers, but are instead the political and sociological responses emerging from a particular conceptualization of disability.

In other words, social model theorists are incorrect in claiming that an interactional model is a misrepresentation of the experience with disability. In the examples provided above by Rioux and Oliver, they are attempting to answer a completely different question than interactional theorists. Interactional theorists are attempting to uncover the metaphysical basis of disability, while social model theorists are engaged in a political activity to promote the well-being of people with disabilities through defining disability in a manner that promotes an understanding that advances their mandate. One camp (interactional theorists) is concerned with a conception of disability that corresponds with reality, while the other (social model theorists) is concerned with a conception of disability that avoids harm being done to people with disabilities.

We can move to one further point that I think the Santa Claus example can help us establish. At a particular point in a child's development, we realize that it is no longer in the child's best interest to continue to allow them to believe Santa Claus exists. Instead, we allow the truth to emerge either through direct intervention or by allowing the child's peers to inform her about reality. We realize that after a child's infancy, we are doing harm if we allow the child to continue to operate in a world where she believes Santa Claus is a real person, delivering presents into our homes and every other home of good children around the world.

Similarly, where the social model once had its place and increased the well-being of individuals in the world, its usefulness has run out. Disability Studies is no longer in its infancy—it no longer requires the skewing of reality to protect and empower people with disabilities.

We cannot begin to move forward in promoting values of justice, morality, and equality for people with disabilities with a skewed conception of whom we wish to promote these values for. Precisely how we go about promoting these values depends on us having an accurate characterization of the experiences of people with disabilities—the targets of our conceptions of justice.

Just like the world of the vast majority of children does not crumble down after they are provided the truth about Santa Claus's existence, disability studies will not fail either. There is another stage ahead for disability studies, and by forcing it to cling to the past we are preventing it from promoting the full rights of people with disabilities.

Concluding Remarks

In other words, instead of moving ahead, social model theorists have been inciting fear in those around them by suggesting that disability studies will fail if disability is characterized in the manner advocated by interactionalists. While it was once a political success and of tremendous importance, I suggest the social model and those who endorse it now risk undoing its benefits. I fear they, like Chicken Little or Henny Penny, are feverishly panicking over very little and inciting fear and worry in those around them.[46] This concern has magnified itself to what it is today, but stems from few, if any, actualized problems.

I believe that social model theorists have engaged in a debate with interactional theorists over the conceptualization of disability when they have an entirely different mandate. Social model theorists insist an interactional model is wrong because it may have bad implications for how people with disabilities are perceived, but disregard the fact that interactional model theorists are concerned with, first and foremost, the reality of disability—figuring out precisely what or who people with disabilities are. Interactional model theorists tend to believe that only after we have adequately wrapped our heads around what we mean when we say "disabled," can we begin to endorse the attitudes about people with disabilities social model proponents are pushing for. Interactional theorists aim to uncover the truth about disability, regardless of what the potential negative political implications may be.

Theorizing about disability from an accurate foundation is imperative for an examination of justice and disability. Without understanding precisely how disadvantage is created from disability, one risks formulating a conception of justice that fails to take into account the many sources and forms of disadvantage that make promoting the rights of people with disabilities so difficult, yet so important.

I hope to demonstrate that it is the complex interaction between impairment (or individual limitations in functioning) and disability (or socially derived forms of oppression) that illuminates potential areas of weakness for the capability theorist. While addressing either impairment or disability on their own might be possible, I suggest that when taken in conjunction, the disadvantage that is created introduces weaknesses in the capabilities approach that, if taken separately, as directed by a medical or social models of disability, would not be present.

It appears that if what I am saying is true, that the interactional theorists are in fact, doing the heavy lifting—they are asking the tough questions to enact real change and to formulate our conceptual basis moving forward. Conversely, social model proponents such as Oliver are asking a different set of questions, with what appears to be drastically less important results for the long-term discussion and promotion of the rights of people with disabilities. After all, interactional theorists are concerned with the reality of disability to ensure that the policies enacted, and conceptual basis' formulated, take into account all of the various forms of disadvantage (both social and individual) for people with disabilities.

Ironically, in an obviously fallacious manner, Oliver suggests that because Shakespeare's work is informed and grounded by philosophy, that it must be wrong. He suggests that "[he] remain[s] convinced that [philosophy's] only use is as a career opportunity for middle class intellectuals who can't get a proper job."[47] He goes on to express how Shakespeare's work is divorced from reality as a result of these ties to philosophy.[48] I think it is reasonable to infer, because the vast majority of interactional theorists tend to be philosophers or to rely upon philosophical methodologies, and because Oliver opposes the interactional framework, that he would conclude the interactional model does little by way of real work for disability.[49]

If what social model theorists are concerned with is the promotion of rights for people with disabilities, I think the discussion above has pointed to the fact that they have a potentially superficial understanding of what it means to be concerned about these rights. By attempting to formulate an understanding of disability that avoids potentially harmful implications for people with disabilities, these theorists are simultaneously guilty of risking the employment of a conception of disability that is doomed to exclude a vast array of disadvantage associated with what the experience of disability actually is. The words of these theorists resonate with many and have been converting many to the beliefs of the social model for quite some time. Unfortunately, they appear to be being led astray.

Notes

1. Tom Shakespeare, *Disability Rights and Wrongs* (New York: Routledge, 2006).
2. Jerome Bickenbach et al., "Models of Disablement, Universalism, and the International Classification of Impairments, Disabilities and Handicaps," *Social Science and Medicine* 48, no. 1 (1999): 1173; Jerome Bickenbach, *Physical Disability and Social Policy* (Toronto: University of Toronto Press, 1993): 12–15.
3. Marcia Rioux, "Disability: The Place of Judgement in a World of Fact," *Journal of Intellectual Disability Research* 41, no. 2 (1997): 102.
4. Michael Oliver, *Understanding Disability: From Theory to Practice* (New York: Saint Martin's Press, 1996), 32.
5. This distinction has been acknowledged to originate from a distinction made in: Union of the Physically Impaired Against Segregation, *Fundament Principles of Disability* (London: Union of the Physically Impaired Against Segregation, 1976).
6. Shakespeare, *Rights and Wrongs*, 34.
7. Shakespeare, *Rights and Wrongs*, 34.
8. Shakespeare, *Rights and Wrongs*, 34.
9. Shakespeare, *Rights and Wrongs*, 34.
10. Shakespeare, *Rights and Wrongs*, 50.
11. Albeit, this claim was made by one of the original theorists behind the social model—Michael Oliver. See Oliver, *Understanding Disability*, 31.
12. Oliver, *Understanding Disability*, 43.
13. Shakespeare, *Rights and Wrongs*, 29.
14. Shakespeare, *Rights and Wrongs*, 30.
15. Shakespeare, *Rights and Wrongs*, 30. Also, see Americans with Disabilities Act of 1990 (ADA), 42 U.S.C. §§ 12101-12213 (2000).
16. Shakespeare, *Rights and Wrongs*, 30.
17. Jerome E. Bickenbach, "Measuring Health: The Disability Critique Revisited," paper presented at the Third Annual International Conference on

Ethical issues in the Measurement of Health and the Global Burden of Disease (Cambridge, Massachusetts: Harvard University School of Public Health, April 24–25 2008).

18. Bickenbach, "Measuring Health."

19. This example is adapted from one of Cohen's originally given in a different context in G. A. Cohen, "On the Currency of Egalitarian Justice," *Ethics* 99, no. 4 (1989): 919.

20. For more on this somewhat peripheral distinction that I did not elaborate upon here, see Cohen, "On the Currency of Egalitarian Justice," 919.

21. Shakespeare, *Rights and Wrongs*, 35.

22. Shakespeare, *Rights and Wrongs*, 35.

23. Shakespeare, *Rights and Wrongs*, 35.

24. Shakespeare, *Rights and Wrongs*, 35.

25. Shakespeare, *Rights and Wrongs*, 35.

26. Shakespeare, *Rights and Wrongs*, 35.

27. Shakespeare, *Rights and Wrongs*, 36.

28. Shakespeare, *Rights and Wrongs*, 36.

29. Simo Vehmas, "Philosophy and Science: The Axis of Evil in Disability Studies," *Journal of Medical Ethics* 34, no. 1 (2008): 22.

30. Simo Vehmas and Pekka Makela, "The Ontology of Disability & Impairment: A Discussion of the Natural and Social Features," in *Arguing about Disability: Philosophical Perspectives*, edited by Kristjana Kristiansen, Simo Vehmas, and Tom Shakespeare (London: Routledge, 2008), 47.

31. Vehmas, "Axis of Evil," 22.

32. Vehmas and Makela, "The Ontology of Disability & Impairment," 47.

33. Vehmas, "Axis of Evil," 22.

34. Vehmas, "Axis of Evil," 23.

35. Vehmas, "Axis of Evil," 23.

36. Vehmas, "Axis of Evil," 23.

37. Simo Vehmas, "Dimensions of Disability," *Cambridge Quarterly of Healthcare Ethics* 13, no. 1 (2004): 39.

38. John Harris, "Is There a Coherent Social Conception of Disability?," *Journal of Medical Ethics* 26, no. 2 (2000): 98.

39. I want to take caution to not overstate this point. Many, if not most, disabilities are contingent, and the primary focus of our investigations should be on social barriers. That said, some impairments, such as the pain experienced from arthritis, are bad in and of themselves. Some experiences cannot be remedied through enacting social change.

40. Vehmas, "Axis of Evil," 21.

41. Michael Oliver, review of *Disability Rights and Wrongs?*, by Tom Shakespeare, *Disability & Society* 22, no. 2 (2007): 233.

42. Oliver, "Rights and Wrongs," 232.

43. Oliver, "Rights and Wrongs," 232.

44. Rioux, "World of Fact," 109.

45. Rioux, "World of Fact," 109.

46. See notes 41–45 re: Oliver & Rioux for examples of the fear and panic I mention here.

47. Oliver, "Rights and Wrongs," 230.

48. Oliver, "Rights and Wrongs," 230.

49. Colin Barnes, another founder of the social model, makes similar ad hominem arguments against a collection of essays edited in part by Shakespeare in: Colin Barnes, review of *Arguing About Disability: Philosophical Perspectives*, eds. Kristjana Kristiansen, Simo Vehmas, and Tom Shakespeare, *Disability & Society* 25 no. 1, (2010): 123. He suggests that the collection, due to it originating from a philosophical perspective, employed difficult, opaque language, and ultimately, advanced nothing of worth for the policy world.

Chapter 3
The Capabilities Approach

Prior to engaging in a critical examination of the capabilities approach, it may prove beneficial to briefly explain both the history as well as the basic theoretical foundations of this understanding of justice.

There of course, have been numerous proponents of this approach. It was first introduced by Amartya Sen who suggested that a focus on the possession of goods or resources was inadequate for the purpose of examinations of justice.[1] Instead, he argued that what really mattered was what people were able to be or do as a result of possessing goods or resources. According to Sen, "the conversion of goods to capabilities [opportunities to pursue various valuable life states] varies from person to person substantially, and the equality of the former may still be far from the equality of the latter".[2] We can see the truth of this statement by examining the life of an individual with a severe disability. The costs of living are often drastically increased for disabled individuals as basic functions such as navigating their built environment come at a much greater expenditure of resources. Therefore, an adequate distribution must take into account what people are capable of doing with the resources at their disposal, and not simply what goods they might avail themselves of.

What Are Capabilities and Functionings?

According to Sen, we must shift our attention from goods or resources to instead, what these goods can do to and for human beings.[3] The primary focus ought to be individuals' capability to function.[4] The capabilities approach has two primary components. Briefly, "functionings" are things and/or activities that people have a choice between. A "capability" is a set of

31

functionings an individual has a choice over. Therefore, one's capability set represents her freedom to choose alternative lives to lead. These capabilities should be pursued by each and every person and the goal of such an approach is to treat each person as an ends, and never as a mere means to the ends of another.[5]

Martha Nussbaum has suggested that "one way of thinking about the capabilities list is to think of it as embodied in a list of constitutional guarantees."[6] One's capability set is the set of *substantial freedoms* genuinely and securely available to pursue. The end state of a realized capability is a functioning. There are various valuable functionings in life and the capabilities approach, at least according to Nussbaum, is resolutely pluralistic about value.[7]

Wolff and De-Shalit agree, and argue first, that disadvantage is plural and is in one sense, a matter of low functioning.[8] Second, they suggest that not only is disadvantage related to the actual functionings achieved, but more importantly, that a vital aspect of advantage and disadvantage is also one's prospect of achieving or sustaining a particular level of functioning.[9] This notion introduces security as it relates to functioning—or security as it relates to achievement rather than merely the ability to achieve. One way of being disadvantaged is when one's functionings become insecure involuntarily (or when one must make one functioning insecure to ensure another). The assurance of "expected functioning" or "expected utility" can reduce individual responsibility however.[10] Wolff and De-Shalit address the need for individuals to be responsible for their actions by suggesting that the idea of "capability" is too vague when attempting to address such considerations, and that instead, it should be replaced with the idea of "genuine opportunities" for secure functionings, thus ensuring individuals are held accountable for their own actions while also providing security.

Various other capable theorists have advanced, defended, or modified the capabilities approach as well.[11] However, I do take Nussbaum's version of the capabilities approach to be primary in this examination, and will return to it now. I focus primarily on Nussbaum partly for reasons of necessary limitations, but mainly because she is far more explicit than most with reference to both the philosophical assumptions and importance of the approach, as well as how this approach addresses problems of disability and health.

Where Do the Central Capabilities Come From?

In her early conceptualizations of the capabilities approach, Nussbaum defended her list of basic capabilities by appealing to a criterion of what it means to be "truly human." More specifically, she asked, "what are the features of our common humanity, features that lead us to recognize certain others, however, distant in their location and their forms of life, as humans, and on the other hand, to decide that certain other beings who resemble us superficially could not possibly be human?."[12]

Take the following examples to illustrate this process. Were we to encounter a set of creatures that resemble humans physically, but that instead, had eternal life, or perhaps did not attach any value to life whatsoever and wanted to die as quickly as possible, we would likely consider them to be so distinct from us because of these peculiarities, that they could not possibly count as human. The fact that we face death, and generally all wish to live, coupled with the fact that we would deem any creature who did not face death or wish to live as being so distinct from us it did not qualify as a human being, gives us reason to include "life" on the basic capability list.[13]

Take one last example to highlight the process Nussbaum used to arrive at her basic capability list. She suggested that we would regard an inability to laugh to signify some sort of deep disturbance in an individual.[14] Moreover, were we to imagine a society comprised entirely of individuals lacking the ability to laugh and find humor in things, we would find such a society strange or perhaps even frightening.[15] Therefore, according to Nussbaum, the capabilities of humor and play ought to be included on the list because they are part of what it means to be distinctly human. Nussbaum offered similar rationales for specifying the other eight capabilities as well.

In shoring up these justifications, she also consistently speaks of living a life worthy of human dignity.[16] More specifically, she asks us what conditions must be met in order to say that one is living a life worthy of human dignity.[17] That said, it is not my intention to justify, defend, or critique the methods employed by Nussbaum to arrive at her conception here. I simply mention such things by way of background for what follows.

Ultimately, through such a process, Nussbaum arrives at a list of ten basic capabilities that are required for one to be living a life worthy of human dignity. They are as follows:

1. *Life.* Being able to live to the end of a human life of normal length; not dying prematurely, or before one's life is so reduced as to be not worth living.
2. *Bodily Health.* Being able to have good health, including reproductive health; to be adequately nourished; to have adequate shelter.
3. *Bodily Integrity.* Being able to move freely from place to place; to be secure against violent assault, including sexual assault and domestic violence; having opportunities for sexual satisfaction and for choice in matters of reproduction.
4. *Senses, Imagination, and Thought.* Being able to use the senses, to imagine, think, and reason—and to do these things in a "truly human" way, a way informed and cultivated by an adequate education, includ-

ing, but by no means limited to, literacy and basic mathematical and scientific training. Being able to use imagination and thought in connection with experiencing and producing works and events of one's own choice, religious, literary, musical, and so forth. Being able to use one's mind in ways protected by guarantees of freedom of expression with respect to both political and artistic speech, and freedom of religious exercise. Being able to have pleasurable experiences and to avoid nonbeneficial pain.

5. *Emotions.* Being able to have attachments to things and people outside ourselves; to love those who love and care for us, to grieve at their absence; in general, to love, to grieve, to experience longing, gratitude, and justified anger. Not having one's emotional development blighted by fear and anxiety. (Supporting this capability means supporting forms of human association that can be shown to be crucial in their development.)

6. *Practical Reason.* Being able to form a conception of the good and to engage in critical reflection about the planning of one's life. (This entails protection for the liberty of conscience and religious observance.)

7. *Affiliation.*
    A. Being able to live with and toward others, to recognize and show concern for other human beings, to engage in various forms of social interaction; to be able to imagine the situation of another. (Protecting this capability means protecting institutions that constitute and nourish such forms of affiliation, and also protecting the freedom of assembly and political speech.)
    B. Having the social bases of self-respect and nonhumiliation; being able to be treated as a dignified being whose worth is equal to that of others. This entails provisions of nondiscrimination on the basis of race, sex, sexual orientation, ethnicity, caste, religion, national origin.

8. *Other Species.* Being able to live with concern for and in relation to animals, plants, and the world of nature.

9. *Play.* Being able to laugh, to play, to enjoy recreational activities.

10. *Control over One's Environment.*
    A. *Political.* Being able to participate effectively in political choices that govern one's life; having the right of political participation, protections of free speech and association.
    B. *Material.* Being able to hold property (both land and movable goods), and having property rights on an equal basis with others; having the right to seek employment on an equal basis with others; having the freedom from unwarranted search and seizure. In work, being able to work as a human being, exercising practical reason and entering into meaningful relationships of mutual recognition with other workers.[18]

I argue that despite the clear strengths of the capabilities approach in egalitarian thought, it fails to provide us with an account of justice to accommodate people with disabilities into our egalitarian framework.

Against Welfare Theories

For the purpose of his examination, Sen took utilitarian principles to be a paradigmatic representation of welfare theories. These utilitarian principles of justice have recently had resurgence in the promotion of rights for disabled persons. This is largely due to Mark Stein's elegantly argued *Distributive Justice and Disability: Utilitarianism Against Egalitarianism*. In his work, Stein endorses utilitarian principles of justice over egalitarian ones and argues that the only manner in which egalitarian principles can serve to adequately account for the experience of disability is vis-à-vis the employment of utilitarian-like principles.[19]

Sen, however, questions the viability of utilitarian principles in the assurance of justice for disabled persons. In Sen's *On Economic Inequality*, he discusses the common criticism launched against utilitarians by egalitarians. This criticism is concerned with the benefits a disabled person could derive from a similar amount of resources as a nondisabled person, and subsequently, the less marginal welfare of people with disabilities.[20]

In his example, Sen provides the reader with two individuals, one of whom derives exactly twice as much utility as the other from any given resource or level of income.[21] The argument unfolds by asserting that one individual's marginal utility is exactly twice of that of the others, and should they be allotted the same income, that this individual would derive twice as much utility from an additional dollar or resource. Subsequently, the egalitarian concern goes, the individual less capable of deriving benefits from resources (or the disabled person), would be excluded from utilitarian distributive considerations by virtue of the fact that maximizing utility would call for the individual better able to benefit from the resources to receive them. This would understandably, compound, and not rectify injustices.

There exist persistent disabling barriers in a disabled person's life that often create an inability or difficulty in converting resources into utility. As a result of these barriers, people with disabilities tend to be less efficient in the eyes of a consequentialist, and thus, less likely to be the recipients of redistributed resources.

In short, Sen rejects consequentialist theories because generally, they tend to rely upon utility as the *exclusive* determining factor when assessing what we owe to each other. This exclusion of nonutility information from our moral judgments results in unfortunate circumstances—like people with disabilities being excluded from our redistributive schemes—that we tend to think are unjust. I am apt to agree with Sen here and think Stein's response, although worthy of attention, does not escape Sen's original critical remarks.

Against Resource Theories

Moving on, we can now examine in a more explicit manner Sen's critique of resource-based conceptions of justice. This examination will be briefer than the last because I believe the claims to be much more self-evident.

Of those we can slot under the heading "The Equality of Resources," there is consensus that John Rawls's work in *A Theory of Justice* is the most influential resource theory from which all contemporary egalitarian debates launch. Like many before him, Rawls is a social contract theorist. Rawls appeals to a position he calls "the original position" to derive an intuitionist account of the various principles of justice that should be chosen or applied under particular circumstances.[22] The aim of the original position is, according to Rawls, "to rule out those principles that it would be rational to propose for acceptance, however little the chance of success, only if one knew certain things that are irrelevant from the standpoint of justice."[23] More specifically, Rawls states that if a man knew he was wealthy, he might see it rational to deem increased taxes to the wealthy unjust. The original position however, is a hypothetical position where one might find herself deprived of this information.[24] Rawls's veil of ignorance, when joined with the original position, allows individuals to "define principles of justice as those which rational persons concerned to advance their interests would consent to as equals when none are known to be advantaged or disadvantaged by social and natural contingencies."[25]

Rawls suggests that two principles of justice would be chosen by those in the original position. The first principle is: "each person is to have an equal right to the most extensive basic liberty compatible with a similar liberty for others."[26] The basic liberties Rawls suggests are, political liberty (the right to vote and be eligible for office) as well as freedom of speech and assembly; liberty of conscience and freedom of thought; freedom of the personal with personal property rights; and freedom from arbitrary arrest.[27] These liberties are all required for one to be equal. According to Rawls, all citizens of a just society must have the same basic rights.[28] These liberties are thus, lexically prior to the second principle.

The second principle derived from the original position is that "social and economic inequalities are to be arranged so that they are both (a) reasonably expected to be to everyone's advantage, and (b) attached to the positions and offices open to all."[29] This principle applies to distributions of income and wealth, and not civil liberties like the first. The first portion of the second principle is identified as the "difference principle." This specifies that departures in equality of primary goods are permitted or justifiable only insofar as they improve the circumstances of the worst off.

Rawls introduces priority rules to specify first, that principles of justice "are to be ranked in lexical order and therefore liberty can be restricted only for the sake of liberty."[30] Thus, liberties take precedence over opportunities, which take precedence over resources. Second, "the second principle of justice is lexically prior to the principle of efficiency and to that of maximizing the sum of advantages; and fair opportunity is prior to the difference principle."[31]

The central observation motivating Sen's push away from resource-based theories was that they tended to "take little note of the diversity of human beings."[32] He believed that resource-based conceptions may do very well in promoting equality if people were basically very similar.[33] Unfortunately, matters are not that easy, and people have many differing needs that vary along numerous dimensions: "health, climate conditions, location, work conditions, temperament, and even body size (affecting food and clothing requirements)."[34] Similar to welfare-based conceptions that have excluded a particular form of need associated with disability from their calculations, resource-based conceptions miss a good deal of the disadvantage suffered by people with disabilities through the promotion of a very narrow conception of what the currency of justice ought to be.

Sen launches a striking attack against Rawls, suggesting he and other resource-based theorists are guilty of fetishism—taking "primary goods as the embodiment of advantage, rather than taking advantage to be a relationship between persons and goods."[35] Sen suggests that "[p]rimary goods suffers from a fetishistic handicap in being concerned with goods, and even though the list of goods is specified in a broad and inclusive way, encompassing rights, liberties, opportunities, income, wealth, and the social basis of self-respect, it still is concerned with good things rather than with what these good things *do* to human beings."[36]

In other words, we need to shift our attention away from the goods or resources that resource theorists fetishize, and instead focus on what goods do to human beings, or what human beings can do with these goods.

Returning to an earlier point, if human beings were relatively similar, this shift might not warrant much attention as a matter of procedure, but I hope it is quite obvious that individuals differ greatly in their abilities to utilize these goods in a manner that promotes their well-being. I think Sen is right when he suggests that the equality of goods could very well be far from the equality of capability.[37]

After having said all this, I hope it becomes apparent to the reader that my move to the capabilities approach is not as hasty as it may have initially seemed. There are in fact, principled grounds for glancing over numerous positions. There remains of course, a whole host of alternative theories that might be examined, but again, partly for reasons of the necessary limitations that come alongside a project such as this one, a central focus that will undoubtedly exclude some positions must be adopted.[38]

Notes

1. Amartya Sen, "Equality of What?," in *Equal Freedom: Selected Tanner Lectures on Human Values,* edited by S. Darwall (Ann Arbor: University of Michigan Press, 1995), 328.

2. Sen, "Equality of What?," 329.

3. Sen, "Equality of What?," 329.

4. Jonathan Wolff and Avner De-Shalit, *Disadvantage* (Oxford: Oxford University Press, 2007), 8.

5. Martha Nussbaum, *Women and Human Development* (Cambridge: Cambridge University Press, 2000), 5.

6. Martha Nussbaum, *Frontiers of Justice: Disability, Nationality and Species Membership* (Cambridge: The Belknap Press of Harvard University Press, 2006), 155.

7. Martha Nussbaum, *Creating Capabilities: The Human Development Approach* (Cambridge: The Belknap Press of Harvard University Press, 2011), 18.

8. Wolff and De-Shalit, *Disadvantage,* 24.

9. Wolff and De-Shalit, *Disadvantage,* 65.

10. Wolff and De-Shalit, *Disadvantage,* 75.

11. The most important of which I take to be: Jennifer Prah Ruger, *Health and Social Justice* (New York: Oxford University Press, 2009); Jennifer Prah Ruger, "Toward a Theory of a Right to Health: Capability and Incompletely Theorized Agreements," *Yale Journal of Law and Humanities* 17, no. 2 (2006): 273–326; and Elizabeth S. Anderson, "What is the Point of Equality?," *Ethics* 109, no. 2 (1999): 287–337.

12. Martha Nussbaum, "Aristotelian Social Democracy," in *Liberalism and the Good,* ed. R. Bruce Douglas, Gerald M. Mara, and Henry S. Richardson (New York: Routledge, 1990), 219.

13. Nussbaum, "Aristotelian Social Democracy," 219.

14. Nussbaum, "Aristotelian Social Democracy," 222.

15. Nussbaum, "Aristotelian Social Democracy," 222.

16. Nussbaum, *Frontiers of Justice,* 74.

17. I acknowledge the perhaps troubling use of the word "dignity" in greater detail at the outset of chapter 5, and additionally, in Christopher A. Riddle, "Natural Diversity and Justice for People with Disabilities," in *Disability and the Good Human Life,* edited by B. Schmitz, J. Bickenbach, & F. Felder (Cambridge: Cambridge University Press, 2013).

18. Nussbaum, *Frontiers of Justice,* 76–78.

19. However, Jerome Bickenbach has suggested, and I tend to agree, that the conception of disability that Stein is employing is inaccurate. More specifically, he suggested that Stein's conception of disability was a "conceptually anemic understanding." For more on this see Jerome E. Bickenbach, review of *Distributive Justice and Disability: Utilitarianism Against Egalitarianism,* by Mark S. Stein, *Perspectives on Politics,* 5, no. 3 (2007): 621.

20. Amartya Sen, *On Economic Inequality* (New York: Oxford University Press, 1973), 17.

21. Amartya Sen, *Development as Freedom* (New York: Knopf, 1999), 62.

22. John Rawls, *A Theory of Justice* (Cambridge: Harvard University Press, 1971), 18.

23. Rawls, *A Theory of Justice,* 18.

24. Rawls, *A Theory of Justice,* 19.

25. Rawls, *A Theory of Justice,* 19.

26. Rawls, *A Theory of Justice,* 60.

27. Rawls, *A Theory of Justice,* 61.

28. Rawls, *A Theory of Justice,* 61.

29. Rawls, *A Theory of Justice,* 60.

30. Rawls, *A Theory of Justice,* 302.

31. Rawls, *A Theory of Justice,* 302–303.

32. Sen, "Equality of What?," 325.

33. Sen, "Equality of What?," 325.

34. Sen, "Equality of What?," 325.

35. Sen, "Equality of What?," 326.

36. Sen, "Equality of What?," 328.

37. Sen, "Equality of What?," 329.

38. For example, take the following two leading alternatives that in many ways approximate the capabilities approach: Richard Arneson's "equality of opportunity for welfare" advanced in Richard Arneson, "Equality and Equality of Opportunity for Welfare," *Philosophical Studies* 56, no. 1 (1989): 77–93; and G. A. Cohen's "equal access to advantage" put forth in G. A. Cohen, "On the Currency of Egalitarian Justice," *Ethics* 99, no. 4 (1989): 906–944.

Chapter 4
The Indexing Problem

After having first articulated precisely what the capabilities approach is, and second briefly justified a focus on capabilities exclusively, in what follows, I argue that despite the clear strengths of the capabilities approach in egalitarian thought, it fails, as it stands, to provide a minimal account of justice for people with disabilities. I begin by highlighting those aspects of Nussbaum's conceptualization of the capability approach that feature prominently in this discussion. I then move to a discussion that highlights both the difficulty, as well as necessity of ranking or ordering capabilities. This consideration is complemented by a distinction I make between *horizontal spectral analysis* (the ordering of a capability among other capabilities) and *vertical spectral analysis* (the assessment of the opportunity or ability to achieve, secure, or perform a particular capability distinct from considerations of the relationship to other capabilities).

Nussbaum's Conceptualization of the Capability Approach

In *Frontiers of Justice*, Nussbaum analyzes the capabilities approach and examines in an explicit manner how it might be conceptualized to ensure justice for the disabled. As discussed previously, she argues that it is possible to specify functionings or activities that constitute a good life and promote "human flourishing."[1] More importantly, identifying a list of central human capabilities, Nussbaum argues that "all of them are implicit in the idea of a life worthy of human dignity"[2] and can become what Rawls refers to as the object of an "overlapping consensus."[3]

In an attempt to establish a minimal account of justice, Nussbaum introduces a notion absent from Senian capabilities—a fundamental threshold level.[4] This threshold allows us to classify individuals beneath the minimal level of functioning as lacking access to the capability in question.[5] It signals the shift away from the focus of resource egalitarians on the quantity of resources, to an emphasis on opportunities for activities or functionings as discussed in the previous chapter. In its basic form, all the capabilities Nussbaum specifies—life; bodily health; bodily integrity; senses, imagination, and thought; emotions; practical reason; affiliation; other species; play; control over one's environment—are held to be constitutive of human flourishing.[6] Elements of a life worth living are, according to Nussbaum, plural and not singular. She argues that one is in error to single out any particular capability as being any more or less constitutive of what it means to flourish as a human.[7] She claims, "if people are below the threshold on any one of the capabilities, that is a failure of basic justice, no matter how high up they are on all the others."[8]

The Indexing Problem

The Necessity of Indexing Capabilities

The first difficulty that emerges from Nussbaum's conception of the capabilities approach is concerned with the ranking or ordering of capabilities within a notion of well-being. Sen acknowledges that a form of what he refers to as "quasi-ordering" is necessary to articulate the relative weight being attributed to a particular capability in the context of an individual's pursuit of flourishing.[9] Sen also discusses the necessity of valuation and ranking in *Commodities and Capabilities* through a notion he calls "intersection partial ranking."[10] It is here that Sen argues that one need not rely upon a subjective perspective of well-being of the sort that might complicate comparisons between individuals. Instead, intersection partial rankings (or analysis that can yield partial rankings to allow policy analysts to effectively situate individuals as being better or worse than other subsets of individuals) might be obtained through the utilization of an objective view of flourishing. More pointedly, "an [objective] view would not necessarily rule out the possibility of interpersonal variations of well-being rankings."[11] I will explore Sen's claim that we can arrive at a partial ordering of capabilities later this chapter after having explored Nussbaum's less complex case.

That said, after having conducted a series of interviews in Israel and England, Wolff and De-Shalit argue that there are capabilities that should receive greater weight when assessing an individual's well-being.[12] For example, they question whether reaching the threshold limit for functionings such as "other species" is as important as reaching the basic threshold for the more rich categories of "bodily health" or "life."[13] While Nussbaum claims there are particular functionings or capabilities within every individual's life that are objectively valuable and necessary to flourish, Wolff and De-Shalit employ what I view to be a very effective example to demonstrate the need for the partial ranking of capabilities.

Wolff and De-Shalit invite us to examine two individuals' lives and to consider whether they are lacking access to human flourishing in the same way.[14] For example, take an unemployed individual doing poorly in almost all levels of functioning, and compare this person to a highly paid trader who does well in every aspect of flourishing except "play."[15] It is because, according to Nussbaum, only an individual with all ten capabilities secured is an individual we can deem to be flourishing, that both individuals fall below the minimal threshold of justice and require adjustment.[16] However, practical concerns would suggest that with limited resources available to redistribute, we should classify the unemployed individual as possessing less well-being than the trader. Nussbaum however, fails to introduce a metric to acknowledge or complete such an indexing.

Even if the example were downplayed so as to not result in such tremendous disparity, I believe the lack of an indexing mechanism remains just as problematic. Consider the same trader lacking the capability of "play" but this time, compare her to an individual lacking bodily integrity or the social basis of self-respect because she has a physical disability and her surroundings offer her little in the way of accommodation. Despite both individuals lacking only one aspect of human flourishing (assuming that a physical disability would not result in an inability to secure any of the remaining nine capabilities),[17] it should be apparent that the disabled individual's well-being is more severely compromised than the trader's, who is unable to exercise her capability of "play."

Wolff and De-Shalit acknowledge the necessity of ranking the various capabilities and employ a mechanism they refer to as "complex evaluation" to provide a more robust classification of well-being. They cite decathlon scoring as a prime example of how to weigh seemingly different events to arrive at a singular conclusion about an individual's overall performance.[18] In the case of a decathlon, the performance being evaluated is an individual's athletic ability. In the case of capabilities, the evaluation is being made about an individual's well-being.

Wolff and De-Shalit claim that in some sense, sprinting is incommensurable with another event such as shot-putting. Nevertheless, this incommensurability does not stop us from assessing athletic ability. Through the complex weighing and computation of performance in all of the various events comprising a decathlon, we can arrive at a singular conclusion about the athletic ability of its participants.

However, it is not my intention to examine this claim in any greater depth here. I simply wish to employ Wolff and De-Shalit's example to demonstrate the necessity of arriving at an ordering of capabilities.

Horizontal v. Vertical Spectral Analysis

The decathlon scoring analogy can also shed light on what I view to be a more serious problem plaguing the capabilities approach. I refer to the ordering of capabilities as the *horizontal spectral analysis*—the ranking of capabilities among other capabilities. Wolff and De-Shalit recognize, to some extent, that a horizontal spectral analysis must occur in order to arrive at a minimally just notion of well-being within a capabilities perspective.

However, what I wish to examine in greater depth is the measurement of particular functionings. I believe the decathlon analogy can also assist us in examining this aspect of capability theory. I call this assessment the *vertical spectral analysis*—the assessment of the opportunity or ability to achieve, secure, or perform a particular capability, distinct from considerations of the relationship to other capabilities. An adequate account of particular capabilities requires factoring in the social variations that impede our ability to properly situate individuals above or below her fundamental threshold.

I argue that our inability to properly complete a vertical spectral analysis is a primary problem associated with the capabilities perspective. Unlike well-being or the living of a life with human flourishing, a decathlon and its events have a predetermined ending after which results are measured. In contrast, well-being is measured and exists as a continual process of reassessment and recalculation of actions and goals.

Therefore, assessing how an individual is performing in respect to a particular capability proves to be more difficult than considering success in a particular achievement such as an athletic competition. Not only is there difficulty in assessing an individual's level of well-being because there is no definite time at which measurement should take place, but additionally, individuals cannot be situated at any particular spot on the spectrum. This is when the notion of a vertical spectral analysis becomes helpful in demonstrating the limitations of Nussbaum's capabilities approach. Figure 4.1 demonstrates how we might situate two individuals, *A* and *B*, within a particular event when assessing individual athletic prowess in the context of assessing overall athletic ability in a decathlon.

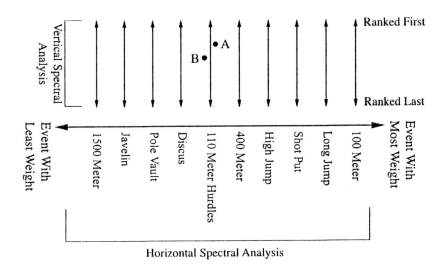

Figure 4.1. Horizontal v. Vertical Spectral Analysis: Decathlon Scoring

In the above figure we can imagine a horizontal spectral analysis occurring that ranked the various events from the event with the most weight, to the event with the least. This has not occurred in the above figure, but we can, for the sake of argument, assume that this is both possible, through a complex algorithm, and complete. What is important to note for the present discussion however, is what is occurring on the vertical, and not the horizontal spectrum. On the vertical spectrum we can note that both individual *A* and individual *B* can occupy only three positions in relation to one another. *A* can perform better, worse, or exactly the same as *B*. There is an inverse relationship of sorts between *A* and *B*—when *A* performs better than *B*, *B* necessarily performs worse than *A*. Decathlons and other similar events are competitive, and one's objective success precludes another's.

This is not the case when examining well-being and capabilities however. First, the attainment of well-being does not necessarily take place within a competitive framework. While one's securing of a capability *might* preclude another from securing that same capability, it is not always the case (and perhaps even rarely the case) that individual *B*'s ranking is compromised by individual *A*'s securing of a functioning.

Second, and perhaps more importantly, people with disabilities exist on a continuum where numerous factors beyond their control impact the chances of the success or failure of their attempts to secure basic thresholds in some capabilities. These include but are not limited to: an individual's environment, social circumstances within that environment, and the particular time in which an assessment takes place. Therefore, unlike the case involving decathlon ranking where an individual is situated at one position on the vertical spectrum and only one position, when examining capabilities individuals occupy a multitude of positions.

I think this is particularly apparent when we revisit the argument advanced in chapter 2 and see that we ought to be characterizing disability as a complex relationship between traits inherent to an individual (impairment) and the social, environmental, and attitudinal barriers (disability) external to that individual. More specifically, after we have pushed away from both a medical and social model understanding of what it is that constitutes disability, and instead, endorse an interactional approach to understanding the experience of disability, we can see that the interconnectedness of an individual and how that individual interacts with her environment seemingly complicates matters a great deal. Individuals have different experiences associated with their impairment based on where they find themselves geographically, the time at which we make assessments, and who they encounter during those experiences.

Thus, instead of situating an individual on the vertical spectrum at one particular point, individuals must instead be placed on multiple points representing the multitude of possible positions they might occupy. These multiple points are meant to signify how volatile the securing of a capability actually is once we have properly understood the varied forms of disadvantage encountered by people with disabilities. More specifically, the experience of disability highlights the complicated factors involved in assessing the potential one has for securing any particular opportunity and how those factors can differ vastly amongst similarly situated individuals. This leads to difficulty in assessing an individual's position on the vertical spectrum even if we can estimate[19] which position the relevant capability occupies on the horizontal continuum.

The problem arises because individuals are no longer in an inverse relationship to one another and no longer occupy only one position on the vertical spectrum; instead, individuals occupy a multitude of positions with the possibility (and indeed, the likelihood) of overlapping realizations of capabilities. As the possible number of positions an individual can occupy increases, the likelihood of overlapping with other individuals increases, as does the difficulty in assessing where to rank that particular individual within their own continuum, as well as in relation to the fundamental threshold.

Figure 4.2 demonstrates what a possible ranking might look like if we were to perform a vertical spectral analysis within a capabilities framework.

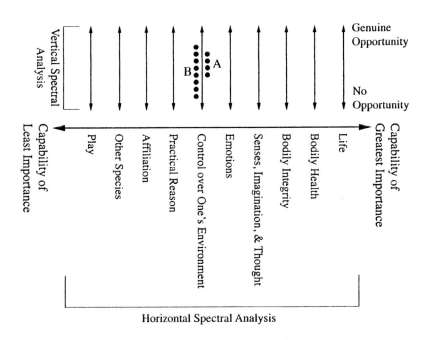

Figure 4.2. Horizontal v. Vertical Spectral Analysis: Ordering Capabilities

In figure 4.2 we can note how both individual *A* and *B* occupy numerous positions along the vertical spectrum.

To examine why it is the case that individuals occupy numerous positions instead of simply one, consider the experiences of an individual with a mobility impairment. This individual may experience less bodily integrity or lack the social bases of self-respect when attempting to utilize public transportation during rush hour when the subway is more heavily utilized than on a weekend. Similarly, she could experience greater pain at some instances in performing different acts that are required of her as a result of her environment. For example, if she utilized crutches to assist with walking and was required to climb a large flight of stairs, this might cause her great discomfort and subsequently, affect her bodily integrity or her social bases of self-respect. Many people with disabilities can attest to such experiences.

The effects disease and health have on individuals and how individuals experience particular impairments differently at different times in their lives are relevant considerations within justice discourse.[20] Thus, the time we decide to assess an individual's ability to secure a functioning is an important aspect in the measurement of well-being. It is not altogether apparent how we might accurately situate an individual at one position on the vertical spectrum when the security of any particular functioning is so volatile. Therefore, I argue that we must place individuals within a continuum (or at multiple points) to account for these variances.

If we examine figure 4.2 more carefully we can see that individual B has a larger continuum (or range of possible positions she might occupy along the vertical spectrum) than A. This is perhaps due to her impairment leading to more significant social barriers, to the impairment being more severe itself, or to the complex interaction of her impairment with her social environment resulting in greater barriers to inclusion, and the subsequent effects on our ability to predict the security of a functioning. While B has the possibility of occupying a marginally higher position on the vertical spectrum, she also has the ability to have secured much less of a particular capability. In light of this, which individual, A or B, should we consider to have secured more of the functioning in question? I argue that the capabilities framework, as it stands, is unable to provide an answer.

If we apply a Nussbaumian conception of a minimum threshold, we arrive at incongruous results. It is likely that in the case displayed in figure 4.2, individual B could reside at, below, *and* above the minimum threshold. It is not apparent how one would assess B's securing of a functioning if B had the possibility of being both well above, and well below the threshold. If our goal is sufficientarian in nature—that is, designed to ensure as many people as possible have a minimally just access to a functioning—and we cannot determine, in any straightforward sort of manner, if individuals access to opportunities are above or below our established sufficiency thresholds, this seems deeply troubling.

Intersection Partial Rankings

Moreover, Sen has suggested that while it may be difficult to offer as precise of a ranking as I suggest is necessary, he argues that we can offer what he calls intersection partial rankings. Intersection partial rankings are utilized to yield a partial ordering from a group of indifference curves. From any given set of indifference curves, we can determine which state is preferable to any other, but cannot determine the degree to which it is preferable.

According to Sen, these sorts of rankings reflect the minimum that can safely be said without any contradictions whatsoever.[21] Sen seems to suggest that while we may not be capable of determining degrees of need, or how much greater one's access to flourishing is compromised than another's, that we can nonetheless make the modest claim that one set of capabilities is preferable to another. Figure 4.3 demonstrates what such rankings might look like.

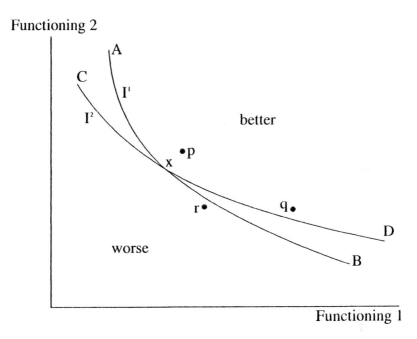

Figure 4.3. Intersection Partial Rankings: Ranking Resources

In figure 4.3 we have two indifference curves, I^1 and I^2, going through x. All points above AxD are superior to x and all points below CxB are inferior to x.[22] More pointedly, points p and q, respectively, are preferable to point r.

The point Sen is intending to make holds if we are referring to the allocation of resources, or other more tangible goods. In the instance presented in figure 4.3, we can conclude that the bundle of goods, p or q, are preferable to the bundle r, but we cannot conclude if p is preferable to q or vice versa. Nor can we conclude the extent to which p or q is preferable to r. Despite the imprecision associated with this method, this, according to Sen, would allow us to make rough estimations concerning need and the allocation of scarce resources to promote genuine access to capabilities.

I am skeptical of how helpful these sorts of rough estimations might be in actuality. Even if these estimations are precise enough for our purposes, I will suggest that figure 4.3 is a mischaracterization of what is required of us in the context of the capabilities approach.

In other words, I do not think figure 4.3 and Sen's suggestions about intersection partial ranking is an adequate characterization of what must be done in the context of the capabilities approach. The capability theorist is not talking about the possession of tangible goods that one can readily make assessments about having access to. Instead, the capability theorist is assessing access to opportunity, and this access, as we have seen, changes for many people with disabilities depending on the context in which they find themselves. I think a more accurate representation of what is required in the context of the capabilities approach is presented in figure 4.4.

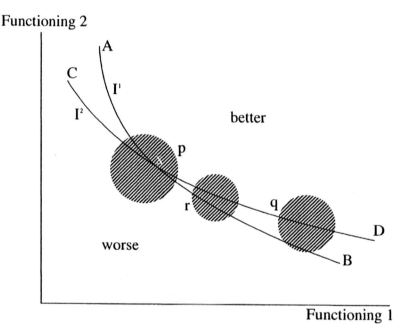

Figure 4.4. Intersection Partial Rankings: Ranking Capabilities

In figure 4.4 we see the same two indifference curves, I^1 and I^2, going through x. We can also still conclude that all points above AxD are superior to x and all points below CxB are inferior to x. However, because p, q, and r no longer represent tangible resources, but instead, states of affairs or the access to capabilities individuals possess, these points are much larger, reflecting the multitude of experiences a person with a disability might experience in attempting to secure a capability set. Here we see that our already generalized judgments become more complex and even more generalized. We can see that the majority of q resides above AxD, but nonetheless, some occupies territory below CxB. Point r resides almost equally above AxD and below CxB. Conversely to q, point p resides almost entirely below CxB, and very little of it occupies any space above AxD. Similar to the difficulties that arose when examining figure 4.2, we can see that it is unclear what sorts of judgments we should be making about access to opportunity, or one's capability set. The capability sets p, q, and r are necessarily defined in a broad way to reflect the ranges of security over particular capabilities experienced by a person with a disability. This is due to, as previously explored, an individual's impairment leading to more significant social barriers, to the impairment being more severe itself, or to the complex interaction of her impairment with her social environment resulting in greater barriers to inclusion, and the subsequent affects on our ability to predict the security of a functioning. The wider the range of these experiences, the larger p, q, or r must become to accurately capture this variance.

In light of the expanding range of possible territories one's access to a capability set requires, and how these expanded ranges interact, overlap, and transcend the established boundaries, it becomes clear that making the sort of assessments Sen suggests is much more difficult than initially suggested. We see that the difficulty in completing a vertical spectral analysis associated with Nussbaum and explored in figure 4.2, is similar when examining Sen and intersection partial rankings in figure 4.4.

Potential Responses

For the sake of simplicity and consistency, let us return to exploring this problem in the context of Nussbaum and figure 4.2. What then, are possible solutions to the apparent inability to perform a vertical spectral analysis with a single outcome that can be analyzed and compared? It might be suggested that one could simply select the mean of all of the possible positions an individual could occupy. Therefore, an individual could be situated at one particular point, reducing the potential overlap between individuals as well as the subsequent confusion in assessing the securing of a functioning. The averaging of the possible positions occupied along the spectrum does not however, secure a level of well-being in accordance to a Nussbaumian conception of flourishing. An individual requires the ability to have reasonable consistency within her life to plan her actions accordingly. Nussbaum places great importance on having the opportunity to plan one's life for both the sake of emotional health as well as autonomy considerations.[23] The only certainty individuals can associate with securing a functioning is that their performance of that particular functioning will be, at the very least, as good as the worst possible position they could occupy along their vertical spectrum. What they are not assured of is the attainment of the average of their possible positions. Consequently, to assign individuals this form of artificial assurance fails to acknowledge the importance of the ability to plan one's life and the well-being associated with it.

In a related manner, one could suggest that we need to recognize that because at any point, an individual might fall to the worst of their possible positions, that the worst foreseeable position is the relevant one for consideration. What this suggestion fails to acknowledge is that the fact that it is a possibility that one may perform poorly at the securing of a particular functioning does not necessitate a complete lack of security over that functioning. Individual B might have the possibility of occupying numerous positions worse than A, but there is also the possibility that B might outperform A. What if B occupied a higher position than A the majority of the time (perhaps even a vastly superior position), but only dropped below A on rare occasions? Would we still wish to claim that B's ability to secure the functioning was less than that of A's? I suspect the answer to this question is "no."

Finally, one might conclude that the degree of variance is the primary focus—an individual with the potential for a diversity of outcomes has less well-being. As mentioned above, certainly individuals require reasonable predictability when it comes to formulating life plans under the capability of "practical reason." Under this metric, B would have performed worse at securing the functioning because B's possible outcomes are more diverse than A's. Consequently, B's ability to predict her outcome or plan her life would be diminished more than A's. I believe that this too however, leads to an undesirable conclusion. Simply because B has the potential to occupy a greater diversity of positions than A does not mean B necessarily occupies a greater diversity than A. A might occupy a new position along her continuum every few hours depending on the nature of her impairment or the disabling barriers she is forced to encounter. B however, may seldom waver from her typical experience. Therefore, it seems inappropriate to hastily introduce this metric as well.

In light of these considerations, I argue that our goal is not only to ensure that the highest possible level of achievement is increased, but also, to narrow the spectrum within which an individual has the possibility of residing. More pointedly, we need to minimize the opportunity an individual has to rank at multiple positions when analyzing the securing of a functioning. This is, understandably, a remarkably difficult goal to achieve. Achieving this goal requires the amelioration of individual impairment, as well as the redressing of social injustices that manifest themselves through the built environment, attitudinal barriers, political structures, and black-letter law.

Without an established metric to successfully determine who is in need, or perhaps more pointedly, who falls below our established fundamental threshold, redistribution and the increase in well-being it might bring about become difficult to achieve. If people with disabilities cannot be situated appropriately on the vertical spectrum, we cannot provide them with appropriate measures to rectify the injustices they suffer.

Thus, the capabilities theorist must introduce a metric to complete a vertical spectral analysis that succeeds where the aforementioned suggestions have failed. She must be capable of determining who resides below the established threshold, as well as the proper means to rectify those injustices once detected.

Concluding Remarks

In what preceded, I have presented what I view to be one of the three primary problems associated with the capabilities approach to egalitarian justice. In relation to the experience of disability, I endorse the finding of Wolff and De-Shalit that the lack of an indexing mechanism will result in tremendous disparities between able-bodied and disabled individuals. Moreover, I contend that we also need a vertical spectral analysis that can take proper account of the nature of disability and deficits in well-being. Without these amendments, the capabilities approach will produce confusion regarding the proper allocation of resources and situating of individuals in relation to a fundamental threshold.

While much attention is now being paid to operationalizing the capabilities approach, this work emphasizes a different aspect of capability theory than what I have stressed. Paul Anand, working in the area of socioeconomics, defends capabilities and demonstrates how one might operationalize the capabilities aspect of Sen's approach.[24] Recently he and other scholars have been part of an international research project designed to further scholarship in this area.

That said, the abundance of work thus far has focused on what Wolff and De-Shalit have called the "indexing problem," that I mention above. Anand and colleagues have demonstrated, and I think convincingly so, that one can "statistically distinguish between different capabilities."[25] Much concern has been expressed over the possibility that different people might weigh different capabilities differently. While continuing work in this area is needed, I believe Anand has provided sound reason to believe this is a concern no longer plaguing capabilities. Although subjective preferences introduce added complexity to the operationalizing of capabilities, these preferences do not prevent us from using a measurement of capabilities as an indicator of well-being.

However, this concern with subjective well-being data does not address the concern about our inability to measure the securing of a particular capability, void of considerations of the relation to either a singular distinct capability, or a lexicographically ordered set of capabilities. In short, a concern with subjective well-being data does not address our inability to perform a vertical spectral analysis. While creating a methodology to operationalize capabilities that can successfully account for subjective variations or personal preferences in ranking capabilities is required, it will not address the concern I have presented here.

The inability to perform a satisfactory vertical spectral analysis is, as mentioned, concerned with objective measurements of capabilities, and not subjective perceptions of well-being. The concern expressed here is not that one might *feel* a lack of control over her environment. Instead, the concern is that we have no objective way with which to measure the actual control she has over her environment because of the great diversity of positions she might occupy on the spectrum. This diversity is problematic because, as suggested above, it is likely that an individual would reside at, below, *and* above the minimum threshold. Moreover, it is not apparent how we might assess the securing of a functioning if the individual in question had the possibility of being both well above and well below the threshold.

I believe Wolff and De-Shalit's decathlon analogy is a useful tool that can shed light on what I view to be an even bigger problem within the capabilities approach. When examining people with disabilities and well-being, I think it is best to compare the ranking of such individuals to the ranking of athletes in mid-event. Any given athlete has a particular "ability," whether naturally endowed or painstakingly acquired. Regardless of race-day conditions, some athletes can simply not perform the task at hand as well as other competitors. This ability, coupled with factors pertaining to the race-day conditions (wind, altitude, temperature, etc.) contribute to the number of possible positions any given athlete might occupy on the vertical spectrum. Therefore, the more apt analogy to demonstrate the difficulties of a capabilities approach and the carrying out of a vertical spectral analysis is one where we attempt to calculate athletic ability, mid-event.

This is understandably, extremely difficult, and for these reasons we should conclude that the capabilities approach, as it stands, is incompletely theorized and requires greater attention to the problems outlined within this section. Determining the degree of need and how to best meet that need is problematic for the capability theorist. Indeed, simply because the experiences of people with disabilities are likely to demonstrate this fact more clearly than those of able-bodied individuals does not indicate that the inability to successfully perform a vertical spectral analysis is limited to people with disabilities. We must reformulate the capabilities perspective to introduce a metric to successfully perform this analysis to promote an adequate minimal conception of justice.

Notes

1. Jennifer Prah Ruger, "Toward a Theory of a Right to Health: Capability and Incompletely Theorized Agreements," *Yale Journal of Law and Humanities* 17, no. 2 (2006): 290–91.

2. Martha Nussbaum, *Frontiers of Justice: Disability, Nationality and Species Membership* (Cambridge: The Belknap Press of Harvard University Press, 2006), 70.

3. For Rawls's original statement on overlapping consensus, see John Rawls, *Political Liberalism* (New York: Columbia University Press, 1993), 128–29.

4. Martha Nussbaum, *Women and Human Development* (Cambridge: Cambridge University Press, 2000), 12.

5. Nussbaum, *Women and Human Development,* 71.

6. Nussbaum, *Women and Human Development,* 75.

7. Nussbaum, *Women and Human Development,* 84.

8. Nussbaum, *Women and Human Development,* 167.

9. Quasi-ordering is an ordering of the aspects of equality that is reflexive, transitive, and incomplete. Sen argues that a partial or incomplete ordering is required because the concept of inequality requires us to recognize that there are many different aspects of well-being that point us in different directions. Thus, a complete ranking cannot be derived from such a notion. When we relate the notion of quasi-ordering to equality, it can be said that quasi-ordering can be classified as a relation of the type: "at least as unequal as." For more on Sen's notion of quasi-ordering see Amartya Sen, *On Economic Inequality* (New York: Oxford University Press, 1973).

10. I discuss the notion of intersection partial rankings more thoroughly below. That said, for more on intersection partial rankings see Amartya Sen–*Commodities and Capabilities* (India: Oxford India Paperbacks, 1999): 22–25; Amartya Sen, *Inequality Reexamined* (Oxford: Oxford University Press, 1992): 46–49; or Sen, *On Economic Inequality.*

11. Sen, *Commodities and Capabilities,* 23.

12. I agree and will address this point in more detail in chapter 6 in the context of health.

13. Jonathan Wolff and Avner De-Shalit, *Disadvantage* (Oxford: Oxford University Press, 2007), 93.

14. In Christopher A. Riddle, "Indexing, Capabilities, and Disability," *The Journal of Social Philosophy* 41, no. 4 (2010): 527–37, I suggested that this is a conclusion to which Nussbaum seems wedded. I now no longer think this is true. Instead, I now realize that Nussbaum says very little about this at all. This concession on my part is not to let Nussbaum off the hook, but rather, to suggest that instead of making an error in commission about this very important point, she has instead, made an error of omission.

15. Wolff and De-Shalit, *Disadvantage*, 101.

16. I think it is necessary to consider that such an example may not be deemed to be a matter of justice to some. One could argue that because the trader had chosen to not foster the capability of play and to instead, promote the remaining capabilities to a greater extent, that no redistribution was required. While this may be true, I believe we can easily manipulate this example to serve the same purpose while avoiding such confusion. Instead, we can imagine two people with disabilities. The first has an impairment that manifests itself in numerous disabling barriers such that she is unable to secure multiple capabilities. The other individual also has an impairment, but does not experience nearly as many barriers. As a result, she is only lacking one of the capabilities identified by Nussbaum. Surely we would wish to prioritize the redistribution of resources such that the individual lacking numerous capabilities would receive greater attention.

17. I am skeptical that such a provision corresponds to any reality and explain this further in my discussion of corrosive disadvantages in chapter 6.

18. Wolff and De-Shalit, *Disadvantage*, 99. It is important to note that Wolff & De-Shalit do not believe the decathlon analogy works completely. Instead, they view this analogy as a step toward finding a solution to the indexing problem, and not the solution itself.

19. Wolff and De-Shalit for example claim that we can make such estimates. See Wolff and De-Shalit, *Disadvantage*, 108–18, for more on this view.

20. Norman Daniels, *Justice and Justification: Reflective Equilibrium in Theory and Practice* (New York: Cambridge University Press, 1999), 196.

21. Sen, *Commodities and Capabilities*, 25.

22. Sen, *Commodities and Capabilities*, 24.

23. Nussbaum, *Frontiers of Justice*, 172.

24. For example, see Paul Anand and Martin van Hees, "Capabilities and Achievements: An Empirical Study," *The Journal of Socio-Economics* 35, no. 2 (2006): 268–84; Paul Anand, C. Santos, and R. Smith, "The Measurement of Capabilities," in *Arguments for a Better World: Essays in Honor of Amartya Sen*, ed. K. Basu and R. Kanbur (Oxford: Oxford University Press, 2009), 283–310; Paul Anand, G. Hunter, I. Carter, K. Dowding, Francesco Guala, and Martin van Hees, "The Development of Capability Indica-

tors," *Journal of Human Development and Capabilities* 10, no. 1 (2009): 125–52.

    25. Anand and van Hees, "Capabilities and Achievements," 279.

Chapter 5
Stigma-Sensitivity

Next, I intend to focus on a related difficulty that arises when attempting to operationalize the capabilities approach. An examination of how the capabilities approach addresses the stigma that often comes part and parcel with justifying redistributive measures that favor a particular "have-not" over other "have-nots" highlights this difficulty. In what follows, I look closely at critiques launched by Thomas Pogge against Nussbaum, as well as the response given from Elizabeth Anderson in support of the capabilities approach.

"Human dignity," writes Martha Nussbaum, "is equal in all who are agents."[1] Everyone is said to deserve equal respect from societal laws and institutions. She argues that the primary target of a theory of egalitarian justice ought to be the protection of freedoms so central that without them, an individual's life is not worthy of human dignity.[2] She argues for the centrality of notions of dignity and respect in articulating a conception of social justice.[3] The conception of dignity at play here espouses a principle of human beings as an end, and not merely a means to another's end.[4]

Not everyone, of course, places such primacy on dignity. Some suggest that while dignity is a notoriously slippery and multidimensional notion, it can retain its usefulness with some further theorizing and clarification.[5] Others still suggest that the notion of human dignity offers little by way of moral justification or guidance.[6] Ruth Macklin, for example, suggested that we can do away with dignity altogether.[7]

A different objection has recently come to the forefront, however. *Contra* those who dissent in the abovementioned manner, this objection acknowledges the importance of dignity, but suggests that the capabilities approach is not the proper means to ensure it. At the foundation of the capabilities approach is the protection of areas of freedom (or capabilities) "so central that their removal makes a life not worthy of human dignity."[8] Thus, dignity plays an integral role in the establishment and justification of the capabilities approach.

The abovementioned objection is not launched because the capabilities approach is thought of as prima facie the incorrect currency of egalitarian justice. Nor is it because the central capabilities thought to be of utmost importance are deemed misrepresentative of what it means to live a life worthy of human dignity. Instead, the emphasis has been placed upon the operationalization of the capabilities approach. More specifically, it has been suggested that the capabilities approach stigmatizes individuals in both the assessment of need, and provision of resources and accommodation, thus undermining an essential aspect of one's human dignity.

In this chapter I suggest that one of the primary measures of the success or failure of a conception of egalitarian justice ought to be its ability to avoid the *further* stigmatization of vulnerable populations when both making assessments of need and implementing measures to address that need.[9] I refer to the ability to not further stigmatize individuals on the basis of naturally acquired skills or endowments when addressing need as *stigma-sensitivity*. I suggest that despite the clear strengths of the capabilities approach, it nevertheless fails to be as stigma-sensitive as potential alternative conceptions. One might deduce (and correctly so) from this statement that stigma-sensitivity is not an all-or-nothing attribute. Conceptions can be more or less stigma-sensitive. While Thomas Pogge suggests the capabilities approach suffers from what he refers to as "the vertical-inequality problem,"[10] Elizabeth Anderson suggests alternatively, that capabilities possess more stigma-sensitivity than resource-based conceptions of justice.[11] My interpretation of the capabilities approach falls somewhere between Pogge's and Anderson's. I suggest this low level of sensitivity ought to be taken seriously within justice discourse and that consequently, we must reformulate the capabilities perspective to be a more stigma-sensitive egalitarian theory in an attempt to promote an adequate minimal conception of justice.

I suggest that when examining competing claims of justice, attention ought to be paid to how we might begin to operationalize redistributive measures and assess need in a society where these values of equality and justice are endorsed. I make a modest and I think, self-evident claim that, when comparing two otherwise equally desirable conceptions of justice, priority ought to be given to the conceptualization that is more stigma-sensitive—that stigmatizes those in need less than other, competing claims. I shall then defend a more ambitious claim, suggesting that strict opportunity-based accounts of distributive justice increase the likelihood of further marginalizing individuals on the basis of naturally acquired skills or endowments.

Acknowledging Need and Difference while Promoting Dignity

There has been a long and rich history addressing the difficulty associated with celebrating difference and recognizing need. This discussion has been perhaps made most famous by Martha Minow. In 1990 she introduced a now famous question she called "the dilemma of difference."[12] More pointedly, the dilemma of difference concerns two interrelated questions. First, when does treating people differently emphasize difference, and result in stigmatization? Second, when does treating people similarly result in insensitivity to difference, and stigmatize and hinder them on that basis? She is concerned that "when we identify one thing as unlike the others, we are dividing the world; we use our language to exclude, to distinguish—to discriminate."[13] This stigma, according to Minow, can be magnified both by ignoring difference, and by focusing on it.[14] Put more simply, the dilemma of difference is a choice between integration and separation—between special treatment and similar treatment.[15] In the present context, the questions are concerned with whether negative stereotypes are reinforced through a commitment to equality, or if on the contrary, differences are accommodated because of the fulfillment of a vision of equality.[16]

In a rather obvious way, there are better or worse ways to go about accounting for difference. The most famous, and perhaps now even clichéd example, is the citing of 15th century English Poor Laws that focused on a distinction between the worthy and unworthy poor. These laws, of course, made people with disabilities the object of pity and charity. This miniature version of a welfare state saw redistribution take the form of local collection and dissemination of resources to only those deemed worthy—the impotent poor: the elderly, widows, and the sick or disabled. Others, who were victims of what we might now call bad option luck,[17] were deemed unworthy of charity and were left to their own devices to overcome the hardships that were perceived to be brought about by their own action or inaction.

That said, I think it is important to bear in mind that, as Carl Knight suggests, "the social stigma of compensation would almost always be outweighed by the benefits of compensation."[18] Anderson acknowledges this point as well when she states, "[o]f course, merely noticing that someone is being unjustly treated can be wounding to the victim."[19] She continues to acknowledge that this is a difficulty all theories of justice will inevitably face. But, "[i]n general, people would prefer that they not suffer injustice, than that their plight be ignored."[20] This point is made of course, not to diminish the significance of stigma-sensitivity, but to instead, emphasize the importance of not *further* stigmatizing individuals on the basis of naturally acquired skills or endowments.

There is an old Finnish proverb that states, "kun menee sutta pakoon, tulee karhu vastaan." Roughly translated into English, this states, "when escaping a wolf, one will run into a bear." This wisdom is of course, meant to suggest that sometimes avoiding one particular danger or undesirable outcome may very well lead to a far worse outcome.[21] I think this adage can lend great insight into our redistributive planning. At a certain point, one necessarily runs a risk of others using an acknowledgment of difference against those the egalitarian planner is attempting to promote justice for. Redistributive measures must be taken which avoid stigmatization, and in an attempt to mitigate that stigmatization and low social standing, what is important is achieving an adequate redistribution while minimizing the stigmatizing effects on the relevant agents. As previously mentioned, my modest claim here is that, *ceteris paribus*, priority ought to be given to the conceptualization of egalitarian justice that is more stigma-sensitive. If there is indeed a genuine risk of stigmatizing individuals through a redistributive scheme, it seems to be a relatively minor one in comparison to the benefits accrued as a result of taking this risk. Put more simply, even if individuals were stigmatized as a result of such a redistribution, it would nevertheless, likely be a favorable one.

Pogge and the Vertical-Inequality Problem

Despite the fact that the stigma associated with compensation would almost always be outweighed by the benefits of the compensation that generated that stigma, it is important to note and promote the most stigma-sensitive conception of egalitarian justice. Put simply, Thomas Pogge thinks we are in error to suggest the capabilities approach is as sensitive to differing natural endowments as alternative approaches.

Recall, Sen suggested a shift in our attention from goods or resources to instead, what goods can do to and for human beings.[22] He suggested that the primary focus ought to be individuals' capability to function.[23] These capabilities should be available to be pursued by each and every person and the goal of such an approach is to treat each person, regardless of resource level or native endowment, as an ends, and never as a mere means to the ends of another.[24]

Pogge has suggested that by making this shift from resources to capabilities, the capabilities approach suffers from what he calls the vertical-inequality problem. Taken in the present context, Pogge would be suggesting the capabilities approach is less stigma-sensitive than a resource-based approach.

He suggests that by shaping institutional arrangements in such a manner that the distribution of resources in society compensates for natural inequalities in endowments, capability theorists are committed to making interpersonal comparisons and judging humans beings as being better or worse than others.[25] He suggests that capability theorists are committed to regarding human diversity in vertical terms.

In the previous chapter I suggested that it is helpful to view the various aspects of the capabilities approach as residing on two spectrums—a vertical and a horizontal. Like Pogge, I thought it was helpful to use the imagery of a vertical spectrum to assist in visualizing what the capability theorist was doing when assessing need. I suggested that assessing need is particularly difficult for the capability theorist because individuals' abilities to secure capabilities cannot be represented as one distinct position on the vertical spectrum. Instead, I suggested that we must represent individuals on this spectrum through a multitude of *potential* positions. Ultimately, I concluded that the capability theorist must introduce a metric to properly assess need in light of the criticism I offer.

Putting aside this skepticism about the ability of the capabilities approach to adequately assess need, Pogge's suggestion is that the very fact that individuals are situated on a vertical spectrum is troubling.

He suggests that the capability theorist must regard individuals as having less or more or a particular endowment, and situate individuals on a vertical spectrum accordingly. He suggests the capabilities approach is committed to viewing diversity as consisting of a natural hierarchy of persons with more or less natural endowments.[26]

Pogge argues that it is precisely because capability theorists have acknowledged that people vary drastically, and that people ought to be compensated for how natural inequalities manifest themselves socially, that they are committed to regarding human natural diversity as residing on a vertical spectrum—in vertical terms.[27]

Conversely, as resource theorists make no such compensatory guarantees, they have no use for the notion of greater or lesser natural endowments, and are thus not committed to a value question in assessing difference. In other words, resource theorists are free to endorse a horizontal conception of natural diversity.

He highlights this distinction with the following example of horizontal reasoning. He claims that if we celebrate natural diversity and acknowledge how our lives are enriched by this variety, we are not committed to viewing the diversity associated with eye color, for example, in better or worse terms.

We can see persons as different without committing ourselves to the view that having brown eyes is better or worse than having blue ones.

Pogge does take a step back to acknowledge that there certainly are some forms of diversity that are, and ought to be, regarded in vertical terms. He suggests that "we speak of bad posture, bad health, and bad memory and thereby explicitly deny that these are no worse than their 'good' counter-parts."[28] He continues to expand this discussion to include many of the things we commonly regard to be worse: "to be dim, obese, balding, frail, tone-deaf, or short."[29] He acknowledges that some of these valuations are cultural, and there are some that we may even wish to eradicate at some point. Nonetheless, Pogge does not suppose that we would wish to be in a world where no one was free to admire or value some particular natural fea-ture of another.[30]

This caveat aside, Pogge does not think that this "partial-verticality" needs to undermine "the shared public sense that human natural diversity *overall* is horizontal."[31] He goes on to clarify further. He claims that musical people, for example, "tend to attach great importance to being musical, and athletes to be athletic, brainy people to brains, and most notoriously—beautiful people to being beautiful."[32] Even though one might admire the musicality of another, one can simultaneously recognize that one has other desirable traits. For example, while the brainy individual might admire the musicality of the musical person, we recognize that the musical person may very well admire the brain of the brainy person, or perhaps the athletic abili-ties of the athlete. Nonetheless, the fact that musical people tend to value musicality reinforces our reluctance to trade or to seriously envy others.[33]

Thus, under a resource-based conception, Pogge concludes that we will possess an awareness of diversity and have a bias in favor of our own en-dowments. And, according to Pogge, "[l]ooking at each person's full set of endowments from a shared social point of view we can sustain the concep-tion of natural inequality as horizontal."[34] Instead of viewing humankind's difference in terms of better or worse valuations, we can instead view it as a wonderful natural diversity to be celebrated.[35]

While resource-based approaches are supported by being able to con-ceptualize diversity in horizontal terms, the capabilities approach, as men-tioned, requires diversity to be understood in vertical terms.[36] By capability theorists affirming that institutions ought to possess a bias in favor of partic-ular people due to a lack of natural endowments, an implicit judgment is being made suggesting that the endowments in question should be regarded as deficient or inferior. The conclusion is often made that not only are these individuals less endowed in respect to a particular form of functioning, but that indeed, they are less well overall.[37] I expand on this point later. But fur-thermore, to add insult to injury, the judgment being made is not simply an expression of a personal preference another individual has, but Pogge claims that the judgment is made from a position of overlapping consensus—from a shared public criterion.[38]

Pogge does concede that this concern for the less naturally endowed is noble, but suggests that this return in thinking to a natural hierarchy, in fact, constitutes a social loss.[39] His concern is that those who are singled out under this compensatory scheme are characterized as naturally disfavored or worse than others. This judgment, of course, prevents individuals from coming forward proudly and insisting on additional resources.[40]

In an important way, we can relate this to discussions about the proper allocation of blame for disability or inability. The argument Pogge is making suggests that blame for one's disability will be put back upon the individual under the capabilities framework, instead of on society, as social model proponents fought so hard to achieve during the early stages of the disability rights movement.

Anderson and the Vertical-Inequality Problem

Having said that, Anderson astutely summarizes the primary difference between resource theorists and capability theorists, and in so doing, summarizes the nature of the debate about stigma-sensitivity. Recall, Anderson suggests that "[t]he fundamental difference between capability theorists and resource theorists lies rather in the degree to which their principles of justice are sensitive to internal individual differences, and environmental features and social norms that interact with these differences."[41]

Resourcism relies upon the basic structure to provide a standardized package or bundle of goods or resources designed to be all purpose means, allowing individuals to realize their particular desired ends.[42]

In contrast, capability theorists call for the basic structure to amend the standard package and to be certain it aligns with differing natural endowments to ensure individuals are not unfairly disadvantaged by requiring greater resources to achieve similar ends as others. These resources are "adjusted to that person's individual ability to convert resources into relevant functionings, and sensitive to environmental factors and social norms that also affect individuals' conversion abilities."[43] According to Anderson, the so-called "hallmark" of the capability approach then, is its "sensitivity to variations in the abilities of individuals to convert resources into functionings, which may be affected by internal variations, environmental features, and prevailing social norms."[44]

We can see by what Pogge has said thus far, and by how Anderson has characterized the capabilities approach, that the primary question dividing resourcists and capability theorists is whether a conception of justice ought to be sensitive to these variations in natural endowment.[45]

Contra Pogge, Anderson suggests that if we think justice requires sensitivity to the diverse natural endowments of individuals, not only in terms of redistributive claims, but also, in terms of avoiding the further stigmatization of individuals—being stigma-sensitive—then we ought to favor a capabilities approach. In other words, Anderson defends the capabilities approach against Pogge's claim that it is not as stigma-sensitive as resource-based conceptions of justice.

Anderson suggests that Pogge has mischaracterized the capabilities approach. I tend to agree with her. She claims that Pogge moves too fast from the capability theorists' concern about natural endowments to a commitment of "attributing the blame for shortfalls in equal functioning to individuals' innate endowments."[46]

In fact, capability theorists view a person's capabilities much more holistically. Here we can invoke imagery from discussions about the definition of disability. While Pogge is attributing a strict medial model way of understanding disability and the disadvantage associated with disability,[47] Anderson is suggesting that capability theorists in fact endorse a view of disability and disadvantage much more akin to an interactional model.

Anderson suggests that an individual's capabilities are best understood as a "joint product of her internal endowments, her external resources, and the social and physical environment in which she lives."[48] This understanding is similar to the current conceptualization of disability being endorsed by most disability theorists. Interactional theorists suggest that disability ought to be regarded as a complex interaction between the traits inherent to a person (or one's impairment), and how these traits manifest themselves in the environment they find themselves in (the disabling facts of one's impairment). In light of this, we can conclude that Anderson, like interactional theorists, vehemently denies that capability theorists must necessarily attribute any failures to function to a presumed inferiority due to the innate, different natural endowments of individuals.[49]

Capability theorists do not hold the position that lacking of a natural endowment, such as high intelligence, is in itself grounds to warrant compensation. Nor do capability theorists suggest that lacking a natural endowment such as intelligence should prompt one to make negative judgments that may stigmatize. Instead, the idea of a capability involves an assessment of how society treats people lacking such an endowment, either through the built environment, the social and political institutions, or the attitudinal barriers they encounter.[50] Therefore, unlike Pogge's claim, capability theorists are not committed to a vertical viewing of natural endowments.

Assessments of Overall Endowment

Thus, we see that Anderson's defense of the capabilities approach relies upon her identifying a mischaracterization of the approach by Pogge. As I stated previously, I think this is an astute observation. That said, I think Anderson has missed another failing of Pogge's that rebuts his critical claims even further.

Recall, Pogge views the fundamental difference between the capabilities approach and a resource-based approach to be the capabilities approach's position on providing accommodation to those disadvantaged in terms of natural endowments.[51] Previously we saw Anderson identify a misrepresentation related to this point. I fear that Pogge has mischaracterized the capabilities approach with reference to this distinction in another way still.

He suggests that in order for an individual to justify her claim as one of justice, she is forced to demonstrate that not only is she worse off with reference to a particular natural endowment than those around her (undoubtedly a move that will result in a diminution of her social basis of self-respect), but she is forced to make a much stronger claim as well. This further claim is even more damaging. Pogge highlights the additional claims she must make by stating, "[i]t is not enough for her to point to one respect in which she is worse off than most others. For there are many other respects in which the addressees of her claim have special limitations, needs, or handicaps, other respects in which she may be better endowed than those she is addressing."[52]

He goes further to suggest that in order for her to have a legitimate claim that she is owed compensation as a matter of justice, "she must present her special limitation, need, or handicap as one that outweighs all other particular vertical inequalities and entitles her to count as worse endowed all things considered."[53]

It is the final clause that Pogge inserts that leads to his misrepresentation of the capabilities approach. In other words, the capability theorist does not invoke the "all things considered" clause that Pogge attributes to her.

Pogge continues by asking: who in their right mind would possibly want to have to claim that their endowments were inferior, overall, to those of most everyone else?[54] Pogge thinks it is obvious that no one would want to be "officially singled out by [their] society for special compensatory benefits reserved for the 'worse endowed.'"[55]

Were this singling out what a capability theorist required for one to receive the special compensation Pogge is concerned with, it would be most troubling and he would be correct in expressing a concern about the lack of stigma-sensitivity displayed by the capabilities approach. Luckily for capability theorists, Pogge is wrong about what is required of an individual to claim special compensation under the capabilities approach.

I will begin by offering general remarks to address what is required under the capabilities approach to justify compensation. I will then move to discuss some more particular characteristics of the capabilities approach that lead me to hold this belief. Before transitioning into my own minor critique of the capabilities approach, I will revisit Pogge's misrepresented version of the capabilities approach to highlight briefly where it went wrong.

In general terms, the capability approach requires no such (explicit) holistic judgment to be made about how a lack of a particular endowment relates to the larger question of overall well-being or opportunity to flourish. This is because the capabilities approach, by its very nature, views all the aspects of well-being that it stresses as being nonfungible and constitutive of living a life worthy of human dignity.[56]

Recall, Nussbaum argues that it is possible to specify the *entirety* of functionings or activities that constitute a good life and promote "human flourishing."[57] Here I added emphasis to "entirety" because Nussbaum argues that all of the capabilities on her list of central human capabilities are "implicit in the idea of a life worthy of human dignity."[58] In other words, all the capabilities Nussbaum specifies are held to be constitutive of human flourishing. Though Nussbaum, Sen, and Wolff's various incarnations of the capabilities approach differ in many respects, a common thread between them all is that they view the elements of a life worth living as being plural and not singular. Nussbaum further characterizes this pluralism when she explicitly states that one is in error to single out any particular capability as being any more or less constitutive of what it means to flourish as a human.[59] The important upshot about this belief is that, "if people are below the threshold on any one of the capabilities, that is a failure of basic justice, no matter how high up they are on all the others."[60] In other words, individuals are not "made to say that [they are] overall worse endowed than others,"[61] as Pogge would have us believe.

Individuals instead can simply rely upon the fact that more generally, a lack of security over a particular functioning is viewed as constituting a failure of basic justice. Individuals in positions like the one described will be granted special compensation, not because they must present a particular limitation as being damaging to their well-being as a whole, but because these capabilities are nonfungible, and that a failure to secure one, for whatever reason, constitutes failure of basic justice. These interpersonal comparisons of well-being that Pogge is concerned about need not arise in the assessment of justice under a capabilities framework. What is more, as Anderson rightly highlighted, capability theorists are not committed to viewing disadvantage as stemming innately from natural endowments, but instead focus on the complex relationship between these endowments and how they interact with the environment, political and legal structures, and attitudinal barriers.[62]

Thus, the onus is doubly shifted away from the individual to express her need in such a manner that justifies a claim to justice. First, she need not express how any special limitation of hers relates to larger questions of well-being. This is because capability theorists are committed to viewing any failure to secure a functioning, whether being solely a result of a special limitation, or as a result of how that limitation manifests itself socially, as a failure of basic justice, thereby warranting redistribution.

Second, in a related manner, in making the assessment associated with a special limitation, capability theorists are not committed to viewing the origins of that limitation as stemming from the individual. Capability theorists can instead view such limitations in social terms.

These two features both highlight how Pogge misrepresented the capabilities approach, as well as demonstrate how stigma-sensitive the capabilities approach is.

Opportunity-Based Perspectives and Stigma-Sensitivity

While to this point I have supported Anderson's defense of the capabilities approach, and indeed, even offered further support of my own against the critical remarks of Pogge, I do not think the capabilities approach can go without criticism.

My criticism can be characterized as one that tends to revolve around a more general observation concerning the broader goals of approaches to justice. More specifically, my concern is that the focus on responsibility that often comes part and parcel with liberal theories of justice may be a conceptual undoing. That said, I do want to limit the scope of my discussion here to strictly focus on capability theory as an alternative to resourcism as I have discussed thus far.

Implicit within an opportunities perspective is a necessary judgment about whether an individual has utilized the resources provided to her adequately to satisfy a basic minimum. This is to say, when we make judgments about the opportunities available to people or the securing of opportunities, we make intrusive evaluations regarding how that individual has lived their life and has utilized (or can utilize) available resources. I contend that this is *potentially* problematic.

Perhaps evaluating the alternative—resource-based conceptions—is a good place to start to highlight this concern. Resource theorists advocate allocating a bundle of all-purpose means to individuals. Most resource-based approaches invest little concern in how the utilization of those resources affect the individual making choices about what to do or not do with those goods.

Contrast this with capabilities approaches that focus on the securing of opportunities. In assessing the opportunities available to any particular individual, there is a backstory that has to be constructed that explains how that individual has arrived at his or her current state of affairs. After all, it is possible that an individual may have otherwise had an opportunity, but opted to squander it in favor of an activity she deemed to be more fruitful. A focus on opportunity involves implicit judgments about the kinds of actions individuals have performed surrounding the securing of that opportunity.

Not only are we making judgments about the background conditions informing one's set of opportunities, but also about the ability of that individual to secure that opportunity. After all, something is not a genuine opportunity if it cannot be secured in practice.[63] So when we ask questions about opportunities, we make an evaluative judgment about individuals' abilities and background conditions informing those opportunities.

In other words, we are asking whether a state of affairs could potentially manifest itself if conditions x, y, or z were met. If these states cannot manifest themselves, we look to the individual (at least partially) to explain this inability.

As Anderson stated before, we do not have to allocate entire blame to an individual for this inability as capability theorists. But the point is, evaluations of this nature, whether focused solely on the individual or not, look to the individual, or her particular circumstances, to explain why an opportunity is not a genuine one. Conversely, there is no such evaluation being made with a starting-line conception, as no evaluations of this nature are being made *ex-post*.

In a distinctive, but I think still useful discussion, T. M. Scanlon has suggested that "[t]he conclusion that a person is responsible [. . .] for what he or she did leaves open what kind of appraisal, if any, is therefore in order–whether what the person did was praiseworthy, blameworthy, or morally neutral."[64] It is this appraisal that Scanlon highlights that leads to a potential lack of stigma-sensitivity. If appraisals are being made that focus on why individual A has a particular opportunity available to her, while B, an otherwise similarly situated individual, fails to have that same opportunity, we run the risk of stigmatizing individuals further. If we praise one for seizing an opportunity and frown upon another for squandering theirs, we risk further marginalizing an already disenfranchised individual. We run this risk because we make intrusive judgments about responsibility and the abilities of the people we are assessing. We necessarily make these judgments because we have to assess the security of an opportunity. We do this to ensure our distribution satisfies our robust conception of well-being.

Concluding Remarks

It appears that a focus on starting-line principles, like those espoused by the majority of resource-based theorists, avoids potential further stigmatizing on the basis of natural endowments or talents. While resourcism is preferable in this instance solely on an stigma-sensitivity metric (due to avoiding opportunity-based discussion), I do not think it satisfies the *ceteris parabus* feature as discussed at the outset of this chapter—it is not otherwise equal—and thus, should not be given equal regard as a conception of justice.

That said, while we have seen that a focus on opportunity leads to a *potential* further stigmatizing of individuals, and that an emphasis instead, on starting-line principles reduces this possibility, we have yet to say anything about end-state principles. That is, what about principles of justice that advocate for the attainment of a particular state of affairs, rather than merely the opportunity to secure that state? I suggest that for reasons very similar to those expressed above concerning starting-line principles endorsed by resource theorists, that end-state principles are also likely to be more stigma-sensitive than opportunity-based conceptions of justice.

After all, if what we are concerned with is simply the attainment of state *A*, and we are directed to disregard all factors pertaining to why an individual was successful or failed at attaining that state, then we seem to avoid the messy judgments that come with opportunity-based discussions. If we deem a particular state of affairs, *A*, to be so valuable that irrespective of the choices exercised surrounding *A*, it ought to be assured, then we run little risk of making intrusive judgments about individuals with reference to responsibility.

In this chapter, I have advanced a principle that I feel should be weighed in assessing conceptualizations of distribution justice. More pointedly, I suggested that one of the primary measures of the success or failure of a conception of egalitarian justice ought to be its ability to avoid the further stigmatization of vulnerable populations. I referred to the ability to not further stigmatize individuals on the basis of naturally acquired skills or endowments as stigma-sensitivity. I suggested that all things being equal, when comparing two equally desirable conceptions of justice, priority ought to be given to the conceptualization that is more stigma-sensitive—that stigmatizes those in need less than other, competing claims.

I then proceeded to examine a criticism made by Pogge that suggested the shift away from resources to capabilities has resulted in the viewing of natural endowments in a vertical manner. Subsequently, Pogge suggested a capabilities approach failed to be as stigma sensitive as opposing, resource-based conceptions.

In addressing this claim, I endorsed a counterremark made by Elizabeth Anderson. I then suggested that in addition to Anderson's claim against Pogge, that he had mischaracterized the capabilities approach in another way still. Thus, the capabilities approach was defended from an attack by resourcism on both accounts: the explicit criticism tackled by Anderson, and the second misrepresentation that lead to an implicit judgment.

Finally, I suggested that while the capabilities approach was not guilty of being less stigma-sensitive for either the explicit or implicit reasons offered by Pogge, that opportunity-based accounts like the capabilities approach do in fact, have the potential to further stigmatize individuals. This is because, among other reasons, judgments about opportunities require an intrusion into individual lives in order to make assessments of the kind necessary to advance an opportunities-based perspective.

Notes

1. Martha Nussbaum, *Creating Capabilities: The Human Development Approach* (Cambridge: The Belknap Press of Harvard University Press, 2011), 31.

2. Nussbaum, *Creating Capabilities*, 31.

3. Nussbaum, *Creating Capabilities*, 26.

4. Nussbaum, *Creating Capabilities*, 25; Martha Nussbaum, *Frontiers of Justice: Disability, Nationality and Species Membership* (Cambridge: The Belknap Press of Harvard University Press, 2006), 36, 70; Martha Nussbaum, *Women and Human Development* (Cambridge: Cambridge University Press, 2000), 74.

5. Doris Schroder. "Dignity: Two Riddles and Four Concepts," *Cambridge Quarterly of Healthcare Ethics* 17, no. 2 (2008): 237.

6. Udo Schüklenk and Anna Pacholczyk, "Dignity's Wooly Uplift," *Bioethics* 24, no. 2 (2010): ii.

7. Ruth Macklin, "Dignity is a Useless Concept," *British Medical Journal* 237, no. 7429 (2003): 1419–20.

8. Nussbaum, *Creating Capabilities*, 31.

9. I owe the emphasis on "further" to Andrew D. F. Ross.

10. Thomas Pogge, "Can the Capability Approach be Justified?," *Philosophical Topics* 30, no. 2 (2002): 204; Thomas Pogge, "A Critique of the Capability Approach," in *Measuring Justice: Primary Goods and Capabili-*

ties, ed. Harry Brighouse and Ingrid Robeyns (Cambridge: Cambridge University Press, 2010), 44.

11. Elizabeth Anderson, "Justifying the Capabilities Approach to Justice," in *Measuring Justice: Primary Goods and Capabilities*, ed. Harry Brighouse and Ingrid Robeyns (Cambridge: Cambridge University Press, 2010), 95–97.

12. Lorella Terzi has suggested that the capabilities framework might altogether overcome the tension Minow raises in the dilemma of differences in "Beyond the Dilemma of Difference: The Capability Approach to Disability and Special Educational Needs," *Journal of Philosophy of Education* 39, no. 3 (2005): 443–59.

13. Martha Minow, *Making All the Difference: Inclusion, Exclusion, and American Law* (Ithaca: Cornell University Press, 1990), 3.

14. Minow, *Making All the Difference*, 20.

15. Minow, *Making All the Difference*, 20–21.

16. Minow, *Making All the Difference*, 21.

17. For more on the distinction between brute and option luck see: Ronald Dworkin, "What is Equality? Part 2: Equality of Resources," *Philosophy and Public Affairs* 10, no. 4 (1981): 293; Ronald Dworkin, *Sovereign Virtue: The Theory and Practice of Equality* (Cambridge: Harvard University Press, 2000), 73–83.

18. Carl Knight, "In Defence of Luck Egalitarianism," *Res Publica* 11, no. 1 (2005): 64.

19. Anderson, "Justifying the Capabilities Approach," 96.

20. Anderson, "Justifying the Capabilities Approach," 96.

21. In an important way we can regard this as being an example of what Wolff might call an inverse-cross-category risk—when steps taken to secure one functioning may put other functionings at risk. See Jonathan Wolff, "Disability Among Equals," in *Disability & Disadvantage*, ed. Kimberly Brownlee and Adam Cureton (Oxford: Oxford University Press, 2009), 120.

22. Amartya Sen, "Equality of What?," in *Equal Freedom: Selected Tanner Lectures on Human Values*, edited by S. Darwall (Ann Arbor: University of Michigan Press, 1995), 328.

23. Jonathan Wolff and Avner De-Shalit, *Disadvantage* (Oxford: Oxford University Press, 2007), 8.

24. Nussbaum, *Women and Human Development*, 5.

25. Pogge, "Can the Capability Approach be Justified?," 204–5.

26. Pogge, "Can the Capability Approach be Justified?," 205–6.

27. Pogge, "Can the Capability Approach be Justified?," 204–5.

28. Pogge, "Can the Capability Approach be Justified?," 205.

29. Pogge, "Can the Capability Approach be Justified?," 205; By no means do I wish to imply that Pogge's list places proper valuations on the things he includes. I simply use his examples to illustrate the intended point.

30. Pogge, "Can the Capability Approach be Justified?," 205.

31. Pogge, "Can the Capability Approach be Justified?," 205.

32. Pogge, "Can the Capability Approach be Justified?," 205.

33. Pogge, "Can the Capability Approach be Justified?," 205.

34. Pogge, "Can the Capability Approach be Justified?," 206.

35. Pogge, "Can the Capability Approach be Justified?," 206.

36. Pogge, "Can the Capability Approach be Justified?," 206.

37. Pogge, "Can the Capability Approach be Justified?," 206.

38. Pogge, "Can the Capability Approach be Justified?," 206.

39. Pogge, "Can the Capability Approach be Justified?," 206.

40. Pogge, "Can the Capability Approach be Justified?," 206.

41. Anderson, "Justifying the Capabilities Approach," 87.

42. Anderson, "Justifying the Capabilities Approach," 87.

43. Anderson, "Justifying the Capabilities Approach," 87.

44. Anderson, "Justifying the Capabilities Approach," 87.

45. Anderson, "Justifying the Capabilities Approach," 87.

46. Anderson, "Justifying the Capabilities Approach," 96.

47. I think this error is similar to one made by Dworkin and highlighted by Shelly Tremain in "Dworkin on Disablement and Resources," *Canadian Journal of Law and Jurisprudence* 9, no. 2 (1996): 344.

48. Anderson, "Justifying the Capabilities Approach," 96.

49. Anderson, "Justifying the Capabilities Approach," 96.

50. Anderson, "Justifying the Capabilities Approach," 97.

51. Pogge, "Can the Capability Approach be Justified?," 206.

52. Pogge, "Can the Capability Approach be Justified?," 206.

53. Pogge, "Can the Capability Approach be Justified?," 206.

54. Pogge, "Can the Capability Approach be Justified?," 206.

55. Pogge, "Can the Capability Approach be Justified?," 207.

56. In the next chapter I suggest that we should in fact, rank capabilities. This suggestion might seemingly undermine this response and instead, inadvertently support Pogge's conclusion. I do not feel this is a necessary feature of my suggestion, however. If we simply create two broad categories of capabilities, as I advocate on behalf of, there appears to be no greater need to demonstrate an overall well-being deficiency to receive compensation. I believe that the points that follow remain sound.

57. Jennifer Prah Ruger, "Toward a Theory of a Right to Health: Capability and Incompletely Theorized Agreements," *Yale Journal of Law and Humanities* 17, no. 2 (2006): 290–91.

58. Nussbaum, *Frontiers of Justice*, 70.

59. Nussbaum, *Frontiers of Justice*, 84.

60. Nussbaum, *Frontiers of Justice*, 167.

61. Pogge, "Can the Capability Approach be Justified?," 206.

62. Anderson, "Justifying the Capabilities Approach," 97.

63. Wolff and De-Shalit, *Disadvantage*, 80.

64. T. M. Scanlon, "Justice, Responsibility, and the Demands of Equality," in *The Egalitarian Conscience: Essays in Honour of G. A. Cohen*, edited by Christine Sypnowich (Oxford: Oxford University Press, 2006), 76.

Chapter 6
The Special Moral Importance of Health

In chapter 4 I discussed the difficulties associated with completing a vertical spectral analysis, while taking for granted our ability to conduct a horizontal spectral analysis—that is, to arrive at an ordering of capabilities. In what follows, I suggest that the capability theorist has failed to provide a conceptual framework to address how one might go about adequately ranking and/or prioritizing the capabilities or a subset of the capabilities Nussbaum specifies—how one might actually conduct a horizontal spectral analysis. I suggest that minimally, there exist two classifications of capabilities, some of which are more important in the pursuit of well-being than others. I take health to be a paradigmatic example of a capability that is of special moral importance. I arrive at this conclusion through an examination of the nature of disadvantage experienced by an absence of the capability of bodily health.

Norman Daniels claims that a theory of justice concerned with health[1] should answer three central questions. First he asks, is health care special? More specifically, what is it about health considerations that result in societies distributing health resources more equally than other goods? Second, which health inequalities are unjust, and when. Finally, in light of health resources being scarce, how can we meet competing interests fairly? Or, how do fairness considerations influence the extent to which health considerations impact the promotion of justice?[2]

In what follows, I intend to demonstrate that health is in fact special. I argue that health plays a special role in the promotion of well-being within the capabilities approach framework. I leave the second question concerning the nature of health inequalities and the third about fairness in the allocation of health resources largely unaddressed.

I proceed by elaborating upon Daniels's answer to the first of his three central questions concerned with justice for health. While Daniels focuses on

Rawls and his social contractors, I focus on the capabilities approach. Despite theorizing from a different conception of justice, my argument for the special moral importance of health bears similarities to Daniels's argument concerning Rawlsian resources and health.

These similarities warrant brief mention. Daniels believes, and I think rightly so, that the idealization of individuals' functioning that often comes part and parcel with classic theorists' conceptions of justice requires redressing. He highlights the fact that Rawls has deliberately simplified his general theory by assuming all individuals are operating as able-bodied citizens in full health over the duration of a typical lifespan.[3] Daniels attempts to show how one could eliminate this idealization while retaining the effectiveness of theories such as Rawls's. He does so by putting forth answers to the three central questions listed above and by asserting that health-care needs are "connected to other central notions in an acceptable theory of justice."[4]

I use this examination as a launching point to examine how the capabilities approach can address topics of justice and health. Ultimately, I suggest that the capabilities approach fails to recognize the special moral importance of health. I do this by first presenting a scenario in an attempt to appeal to our intuitions concerning this position. Second, I initiate a discussion concerning well-being and the nature of disadvantage, designed to further support this position, and to add content to our intuitions.

Is Health Special? The Moral Importance of Health

Prior to moving to a discussion of capabilities, let us briefly examine how Daniels has conceptualized his answer to the first of the three questions of justice for health: is health special? Daniels's answer is supported by what he calls an opportunity-based account.[5]

In his seminal work *Just Health Care*, he argues that health-care needs hold special moral importance since: (1) Health care promotes normal functioning,[6] and normal functioning assures opportunity. Thus, health care promotes opportunity. (2) Since justice requires the promotion of equal opportunities, special moral importance is given to health.[7] More specifically, "the special moral importance of health [care] derives from its impact on our opportunities".[8] The primary goal of health care to is assure normal functioning.[9]

Daniels's recent work has extended his arguments made in *Just Health Care* in at least two important ways. First, he recognizes that health needs generally, and not just health care, are important. This is largely because of the recognition of the abundance of social determinants of health, which according to Daniels,[10] health care is but one. Second, he offers further support for the claims he makes concerning the obligation of justice to protect opportunity.

Daniels's revised central argument in *Just Health* integrates these two thoughts and looks like the following: (1) Meeting health needs promotes normal functioning, which in turn, protects opportunity. Thus, assuring health needs assures opportunity. (2) Since Rawls, Sen, and other distributive justice theorists require the protection of opportunity, health is of special moral importance to justice.[11]

The Intuitive Appeal

I argue that it is only after we have adequately explained why central health capabilities hold special moral importance that the capabilities approach can begin to fully promote justice. I previously presented how Norman Daniels famously took up this question in his 1985 book titled *Just Health Care*, and in 2008 revised his theory in *Just Health*.

Picking up where he left off, Jennifer Prah Ruger, in her *Health and Social Justice*, outlines the theoretical foundations of health capabilities. She stresses that the principles she advances in her work are principles "rooted in . . . human flourishing, which values health intrinsically and more highly than non-intrinsic or solely instrumental social goods, such as income."[12] She suggests that this is where the special moral importance of health is derived. Ruger acknowledges that central health capabilities are special and have moral and practical importance.

I aim to elaborate upon this notion and suggest that a more nuanced argument might help us shore up the claim that special attention ought to be paid to health within a capabilities framework. A good place to start is by making an intuitive appeal.

If we imagine two scenarios, scenario *A* involving an individual experiencing disadvantage due to a failure to secure the capability of health, and scenario *B* involving an individual failing to secure the capability of bodily integrity, but living in good health, I hope the special moral importance of health will become clear. In scenario *A*, the individual has the opportunity to live a healthy lifestyle, but instead chooses to consume far too many fatty foods, to live a sedentary lifestyle, to smoke frequently, to drink excessively, or to engage in any of the other innumerable unhealthy activities one can engage in. All this activity (or inactivity) is done in the face of state health campaigns and publicly sponsored programs to assist in their avoidance (or assurance). Despite the fact that this individual was provided with more than an adequate opportunity to be healthy, he is not. As a result of his choices, he possesses less well-being than another individual who is in all other facets similar, but in good health.

Moving on, the second scenario involves the examination of the life of a monk, generally doing well at securing most of the specified capabilities (thereby possessing the various functionings that correspond with these capabilities). He is however, celibate.[13] According to Nussbaum, sexual or romantic pleasures are things all individuals ought to have a genuine opportunity to pursue. These sorts of pleasures are included in the category of "Bodily Integrity" and Nussbaum indicates that to live a life worthy of human dignity, one must have adequate opportunities for sexual satisfaction.[14] What is important to note in the case of the monk is that he can attain a good life—one worthy of human dignity—whilst being celibate. Provided the monk had a genuine opportunity to enter into meaningful sexual and romantic relationships, and has after deliberation, opted to forgo this opportunity and live a monkish lifestyle, we would not, at least without considerable deliberation and further information being made available to us, say that his life is going poorly, or that he possesses less well-being than another who pursues these sorts of relationships and is otherwise similar.

These two scenarios can make obvious the distinction I aim to put forth. Both scenarios demonstrate the need to offer opportunities for the securing of all functionings—a position all capabilities theorists find appealing. In Scenario *B*, functionings such as bodily integrity, or more specifically, the ability to enter into meaningful sexual and romantic relationships, are highlighted and we rightly conclude that these sorts of things or states of being are desirable, and that all individuals ought to have an opportunity to pursue them. Scenario *B* also highlights that were someone to opt out of these sorts of functionings, their life would not be going less well than another who seized the opportunity to secure the functioning. This is to say, we do not think the monk's life is going less well because he has opted out of securing these functionings. He had the capability of bodily integrity, but opted not to realize the opportunity in the context of his pledged celibacy.

Another example of a functioning of this sort is having political control over one's environment. Nussbaum suggests that having the opportunity "to participate effectively in political choices that govern one's life"[15] is required to flourish. Certainly all individuals ought to have the opportunity to shape their political environment, but were an individual to opt to abstain from voting, for example, I think it is in error to suggest that she possesses less well-being than another who is politically active. Simply assuring the capability to function in this manner is all that is required.

Conversely, in the case of the individual living in poor health, his life is going less well. If one lacks a functioning like bodily health, one possesses less well-being than another similarly situated individual, who was living in good health. In the instance of the capability of bodily health, unlike the ability to pursue meaningful sexual and romantic relationships, or to participate politically, without a securing of the capability, one does possess less well-being.

Our intuitions tend to align with this conclusion when we look at the above scenarios. In both scenario *A* and *B*, the individuals have the opportunity to pursue all valuable functionings, but have opted to abstain from securing one each. In scenario *A*, the individual has opted to lead a lifestyle that has resulted in poor health. In scenario *B*, the individual has opted out of meaningful sexual and romantic relationships. While both scenarios involve the failure to secure only one of the ten capabilities[16] Nussbaum specifies, we tend to conclude the individual in scenario *A '*—the unhealthy individual—possesses less well-being than the monk. We think this is the case because of how we view the disadvantage associated with a failure to secure the functionings in question. More specifically, the monk does not suffer disadvantage as a result of failing to enter into meaningful sexual and romantic relationships, whereas the unhealthy individual does.

It is of course, possible for one to make a well-reasoned case to suggest that the monk or politically apathetic individual do in fact, suffer disadvantage. They suffer disadvantages associated with a failure to realize one's reproductive rights,[17] to experience the intimacy associated with a meaningful sexual relationship, or to be engaged civically in enacting change in one's own society. I am not terribly sympathetic to such claims, but if pressed I would respond in the following manner: even if we grant that these individuals may very well suffer disadvantage, that disadvantage is not comparable to the disadvantage suffered by the individual living in poor health. I suggest this because I view the disadvantage suffered in the absence of good health to be of a different *kind* than the disadvantage (if indeed disadvantage is experienced) suffered as a result of opting out of meaningful sexual and romantic relationships. Why is this the case?

Corrosive Disadvantage

As Sen has acknowledged, living in poor health adversely affects one's ability to secure other capabilities. He distinguishes between a subset of capabilities called "basic capabilities," and other capabilities deemed to be of less importance.[18] Basic capabilities are prerequisites for other, less basic, capabilities. I argue that this distinction, after having been elaborated upon, can form the basis of the special moral importance of health.

The types of disadvantage suffered by one living in poor health affects countless other aspects of that individual's life. The types of disadvantage suffered by an individual lacking a functioning, such as the celibate monk, are not corrosive. In other words, the lack of sexual relationships in the monk's life does not adversely affect his ability to pursue life plans, or to secure any of the other nine functionings. The term "corrosive disadvantage" utilized here is meant to refer to disadvantage that negatively impacts the securing of other valuable things. One may very well suffer disadvantage from failing to secure a valuable thing, but that disadvantage is only corrosive when it reaches into other aspects of that individual's life and negatively impacts the ability to secure other valuable states of being. In other words, as Daniels has argued in the context of Rawlsian primary goods, health is a necessary condition for all other opportunities. In the context of capabilities, we can argue that health resides in a special category of capabilities that are necessary conditions for other capabilities.

This observation seems to suggest that minimally, we ought to be capable of parsing the capabilities Nussbaum specifies into two rough categories[19]—those whose failure to be secured results in the introduction of corrosive disadvantage into one's life; and those whose failure to be secured has little or no impact on one's ability to pursue the remaining capabilities.

If we examine the nature of the hardship experienced by the monk in scenario B in further depth, we can add content to our intuition that he does not suffer a compromise to his well-being in the same sort of manner as the unhealthy individual. Let us examine each of the other nine capabilities systematically.

One's ability to "live to the end of a human life of normal length"[20] is not impacted as a result of a failure to engage to meaningful sexual and romantic relationships. Nor does a monkish lifestyle impact one's ability to live a healthy life, to be adequately nourished, or more generally, to possess the functioning of "Bodily Health." This lifestyle choice has no impact on the freedom one has to utilize their "Senses, Imagination, and Thought," otherwise we would be forced to conclude that children had no freedom to utilize their senses or imagination (yet we often view children to be among the most free to realize this capability).

In a rather obvious way, the monk's emotional development is not hindered. Celibacy does not impact one's ability to form emotional connections with people and to "experience longing, gratitude, and justified anger."[21] It may, of course, limit the amount of people we might feel these emotions towards, but so many of our daily activities do this to such a minor extent (e.g., take the decision to live in a rural community with fewer people over the choice to live in an urban environment with a greater population and thus, a higher probability of interacting on more occasions), that I do not think we would like to include this impact as something that justice considerations should take up. A monk's ability to form a conception of the good is equality as unhindered.

Furthermore, abstaining from sexual activity does not impact one's ability to realize the capability of "Affiliation." It does not change one's ability to "imagine the situation of another" or to "engage in various forms of social interaction," nor does it negatively affect one's "having the social bases of self-respect and nonhumiliation."[22] Similarly, a monkish lifestyle does not affect one's capability of 'Other Species'—one's ability to live with nonhuman animals or in nature and to show concern to the natural world or from being able to enjoy recreational activities—from engaging in "Play."

Finally, the monkish lifestyle does not adversely impact one's ability to have "Control over One's Environment." One can still participate equally as effectively in the political realm in shaping the institutions that govern one's society, as well as in the material realm—one is still free to be able to hold property.

Next, let us examine the nature of disadvantage one incurs if one falls into poor health as the individual in scenario *A* has. First, poor health conditions are I think rather obviously, often the case of premature death. Thus, in the most relevant way possible perhaps, failing to possess "Bodily Health" drastically impacts one's ability to realize the capability of "Life." Similarly, living in poor health negatively impacts one's ability to secure "Bodily Integrity." An unfortunate and startling reality is that those living in poor health or with a disability are far more susceptible to both physical as well as sexual abuse.[23]

Moving on, being in poor health may or may not affect one's ability to realize the capability of "Senses, Imagination, and Thought." Seeing as health is such a multidimensional concept, theorizing in the abstract as I have been doing does not provide us with enough evidence to suggest an impact one way or another. Nonetheless, we can still make a conclusion that advances the intended point. I hope that it is clear to the reader that poor health has the potential to impact the securing of this capability, while abstaining from sexual and romantic relationships does not.

While being unhealthy can be extremely emotionally taxing on individuals, it does not appear to result in one's emotional development being blighted by fear or anxiety in most instances. Similarly, in most instances it seems to be the case that poor bodily health does not impact one's ability to form a conception of the good. It of course, impacts one's ability to pursue that conception, but nonetheless, does not, in most instances, affect one's ability to plan one's life. In some instances however, it may result in such variance in one's day-to-day life that it does negatively impact one's ability to plan one's own life. Many people with disabilities who experience poor health comment on how unpredictable their lives are due to a reliance on caregivers, as well as being impacted and prevented from performing desired functions by the built environment, or attitudinal barriers.

Although poor bodily health does not negatively affect one's ability to empathize or to live with and toward others, being unhealthy leads to a potential to lack the social bases of self-respect and nonhumiliation. We see this in patients who experience the stigmatizing effects of living with HIV, for example. In other words, living an unhealthy lifestyle appears to at least have the potential to negatively influence one's ability to secure the capability of "Affiliation." That said, poor health does not typically appear to negatively impact the securing of the capability of "Other Species" but it may very well impact your ability to enjoy recreational activities or to secure the capability of "Play."

Finally, in a similar vein to the previous point, poor health might influence one's ability to shape the political environment they find themselves in. It might similarly, affect one's ability to "seek employment on an equal basis with others"[24] (i.e., discrimination against HIV-positive patients in the workplace, or a reluctance by employers to hire an individual who requires various forms of accommodation). Thus, while not terribly conclusive, or certainly not a necessary fact associated with a lack of the capability of bodily health, living in poor health might affect one's "Control over One's Environment."

Therefore, even if we were to conclude that the monk does suffer disadvantage as a result of his choice to remain celibate, it is clear that our intuitions about the individual living in poor health being worse off are grounded in an observation about the nature of disadvantage experienced by these two individuals.

Through an examination of how a failure to secure bodily health impacts the securing of the other nine capabilities, it has become clear that health is drastically different from a perspective concerned about well-being, than the ability to engage in meaningful romantic sexual and romantic relationships.

I will not proceed to outline the relationships among the other eight capabilities as I hope that by demonstrating that there is such a sharp contrast in the nature of disadvantage suffered between the two capabilities examined, that we can minimally, conclude that health ought to receive different regard in the promotion of well-being within the capabilities framework than other capabilities.[25]

Concluding Remarks

Health is of special moral importance because of the nature of disadvantage suffered when one lacks the capability of bodily health. Disadvantage is corrosive if it adversely impacts one's ability to secure other valuable functionings. As I have stated elsewhere, Nussbaum has been steadfast in her assertion that "one is in error to single out any particular capability as being any more or less constitutive of what it means to flourish as a human."[26]

If we are concerned with the capabilities approach adequately promoting well-being, then it would seem as if we need to shift from thinking that the capabilities specified are nonfungible and of equal moral worth, to a position that suggests that some capabilities are more important to human flourishing and well-being.

In what preceded, I attempted to argue that the reason the capability of health was so integral to the promotion of well-being was because of the corrosive disadvantage one suffers from a lack of bodily health. I have not suggested that because health has special moral importance that it ought to receive lexicographical priority. I reserve judgments of this nature for a future discussion.

This brief disclaimer aside, I hope it suffices to say that if we aim to uphold justice to encourage human flourishing and to promote well-being within the capabilities approach, we need to recognize the special moral importance of health. This is something that Nussbaum has failed to do, and that others have only sketchily done.

Notes

1. While I recognize there is an incredibly rich discussion of what constitutes health, in keeping with other aspects of this piece I will follow Norman Daniels's conception of health and I will refrain from engaging in a more thorough examination of the possible conceptualizations of health beyond the discussion that follows.

In *Just Health: Meeting Health Needs Fairly* (New York: Cambridge University Press, 1985), Daniels suggests a shift away from two misunderstandings of health. The first is that health is the absence of disease. This is because, of course, the notion of "disease" is too narrow to capture all that we aim to capture when discussing health. Daniels also pushes away from the World Health Organization (WHO) definition that states that "health is a state of complete physical, mental, and social well-being, and not merely the absence of disease or infirmity" (WHO, 1946). I think Daniels is correct when he states that the WHO conception risks turning all disadvantage into health. More recently, Venkatapuram's conception of health advanced in his *Health Justice: An Argument from the Capabilities Approach* (Cambridge: Polity Press, 2011) seems to, in a similar manner, commit us to a somewhat vacuous conception of health, categorizing any deprivation of the central capabilities as being the result of poor health. Instead of relying upon a subjective account of health like the WHO's or Venkatapuram's, which seems incompatible with an objective theory of the good life (e.g., the capabilities approach), Daniels relies upon an objective understanding. He suggests that health should be understood as the absence of pathology (Daniels, New York: Cambridge University Press, 2008). Here we are to understand "pathology" to refer to deviations from species typical functioning. I also favor this understanding of health because of the implications that follow from how health relates to disability (i.e., not all people with disabilities are unhealthy). While this conception may itself be too broad of a notion of health, I do want to leave such disagreement to the sideline for the time being.

It is important to note that one might conflate disability and ill health at this point. This is certainly not my intention. While there often exists a relationship between good health and what Lawrence Becker would call "reliably competent functioning" in his *Habilitation, Health, and Agency* (Oxford: Oxford University Press, 2012), there most certainly is not a necessary connection between the two. While those who are unhealthy often experience functional limitations or impairments that manifest as a disability socially, this is not always the case. One who is poorly nourished would be deemed unhealthy, but this need not cause a functional limitation or impairment, and thus, not a disability. Conversely, while one might be disabled with paraplegia, we certainly would not conclude that paraplegic athletes with an absence of disease are unhealthy. I make this point to suggest that the discussion contained within this chapter should be taken to refer to those in ill health, and to those who are disabled, but to imply no necessary correlation between the two.

2. Norman Daniels, *Just Health Care* (New York: Cambridge University Press, 1985); Norman Daniels, *Justice and Justification: Reflective Equilibrium in Theory and Practice* (New York: Cambridge University Press, 1999); Norman Daniels, "Justice, Health, and Health Care," *American Journal of Bioethics* 1, no. 2 (2001): 2–16; Norman Daniels, *Just Health: Meeting Health Needs Fairly* (New York: Cambridge University Press, 2008).

3. Daniels, "Justice, Health, and Health Care." See John Rawls, *Political Liberalism* (New York: Columbia University Press, 1993); 20–21; and John Rawls, *A Theory of Justice* (Cambridge: Harvard University Press, 1971), 506; for examples of this.

4. Daniels, *Just Health Care*, 19.

5. Daniels, *Just Health Care*, 19.

6. Daniels's notion of functioning differs from the functionings that are components of the capabilities approach and discussed in further detail in chapter 3.

7. Daniels, *Just Health*, 19.

8. Daniels, *Just Health*, 27.

9. Daniels, "Justice, Health, and Health Care," 2.

10. Daniels, *Just Health*, 30.

11. Daniels, *Just Health*, 30. Of course there may be other opportunity protectors that are important as a matter of justice, and we need not concern ourselves with a lexicographical ordering of these for the time being. As I argue in the section titled "Corrosive Disadvantage," I suspect that we can create at least two classifications of capabilities. I suggest that health resides in the category of capabilities that should be given special moral importance over the other class. I thank an anonymous reviewer at *Topoi* for this nuanced point.

12. Jennifer Prah Ruger, *Health and Social Justice* (New York: Oxford University Press, 2009), 3.

13. I first encountered the example of celibacy and monks in Richard Arneson, "'Good Enough' is not Good Enough," in *Capabilities Equality: Basic Issues and Problems*, edited by Alexander Kauffman (New York: Routledge, 2005), 26.

14. Martha Nussbaum, *Creating Capabilities: The Human Development Approach* (Cambridge: The Belknap Press of Harvard University Press, 2011), 33.

15. Martha Nussbaum, *Frontiers of Justice: Disability, Nationality and Species Membership* (Cambridge: The Belknap Press of Harvard University Press, 2006), 77.

16. Here I ignore the likelihood that the absence of some capabilities tends to exclude the possibility of the securing of other capabilities. I assume, counterfactually, that capabilities operate on distinct plains, where an absence of one has no negative (or positive impact) on the others.

17. I would like to thank Jerome Bickenbach for making this suggestion.

18. Amartya Sen, "Capability and Well-Being," in *The Quality of Life*, ed. Martha Nussbaum and Amartya Sen (Oxford: Oxford University, 1993): 30–53.

19. It is important to note that the claim being made is that health has special moral importance. This claim does not exclude the fact that other capabilities might also reside in the category of things with special moral importance. The capability of "bodily health" is simply being used as an example of a capability that resides in a subset of capabilities that Nussbaum fails to acknowledge as requiring special attention. Certainly the corrosiveness of capabilities resides on a spectrum that is difficult to measure definitely. That said, I employ the two examples of health and celibacy to point to two obvious cases of disadvantage: one that prompts justice considerations, and another that does not. One could point to other capabilities that are more difficult to classify as residing in the subset of capabilities that result in

corrosive disadvantage if not secured. Thus, further work is required on establishing what threshold is employed to classify capabilities. This further work is not conducted in this text. Nonetheless, I suspect the original point holds that there are some disadvantages that prompt justice considerations because of the corrosiveness of that disadvantage, and there are some forms of disadvantage that do not. Poor bodily health results in disadvantage that warrants concern in the realm of justice, whilst the disadvantage suffered by celibacy does not. The point being made here concerns the fact that we need to distinguish between classes of disadvantage that result from the absence of a functioning, and not a question about how we should go about parsing the capabilities.

20. Nussbaum, *Frontiers of Justice*, 76.

21. Nussbaum, *Frontiers of Justice*, 77.

22. Nussbaum, *Frontiers of Justice*, 77.

23. For two of the many research projects that affirm this, see: David Alan. Nibert et al., "Assaults against Residents of a Psychiatric Institution: Residents' History of Abuse,""*Journal of Interpersonal Violence* 4, no. 3 (1989): 342–349; or Statistics Canada, Centre for Justice Statistics, "Wife Assault: The Findings of a National Survey,""*Juristate: Service Bulletin* 14, no. 9 (1994).

24. Nussbaum, *Frontiers of Justice*, 77.

25. At this point one might be inclined to suggest that the importance of health might be exaggerated. Take for example Michel Petrucciani. Petrucciani was a famous jazz pianist who died at age thirty-six and suffered from a very substantial disability. One could reasonably conclude that he would not have traded his art for a longer or healthier life. Examples of people sacrificing bodily health for their art are abundant. Maybe we can view the Petrucciani example and other cases like it as evidence that health need not always trump other goods. I suspect this might be a reasonable claim. That said, if we continue to operate within the confines of the capabilities approach we can see that while this claim might be a distinct critique of capabilities, I do not feel it is a refutation of my intended point. I am operating within the parameters set by the capabilities approach. These parameters state, among other things, that the goal of justice should be to maximize the number of capabilities one has a minimally just level of access to. This implies that a capability that minimizes the amount of capabilities one has a minimally just level of access to is particularly important. It has special importance because without it, other capabilities are more difficult to secure. If the goal of the capabilities approach is to maximize the number of capabilities one has minimal access to, then the argument being advanced in this work—that health resides in a class of capabilities that have special moral importance because of the corrosive disadvantage that results from a failure

to secure a healthy life—seems to follow. The critique concerning the exaggeration of the importance of health seems to suggest that the antecedent of the previous claim—that the goal of justice is to maximize the number of capabilities one has minimal access to—is false. This is a distinct critique of the capabilities approach, and not a direct critique of the remarks being made here that assume the antecedent is true and offer critical remarks of the capabilities approach that grant its design is correct, whilst suggesting that its implementation is troubled. Much gratitude is owed to Jerome Bickenbach and Sara Rubinelli for helping me clarify my thoughts on this matter.

26. Christopher A. Riddle, "Measuring Capabilities: The Case of Disability," in *The Capability Approach on Social Order*, edited by Niels Weidtmann, Yanti Martina Hölzchen, and Bilal Hawa (preface by Martha Nussbaum) (Munster: LIT Verlag, 2012), 51; Christopher A. Riddle, "Indexing, Capabilities, and Disability," *The Journal of Social Philosophy* 41, no. 4 (2010): 527–537.

Chapter 7
Capabilities and Disability

"...justice is everywhere and it's working..."

Charles Bukowski, *One for the Shoeshine Man*

My explicit goal in this book was to offer a critical engagement with the capabilities approach that utilized disability as a case study. Or more specifically, to utilize Sen's terminology, I have engaged in a case-implication critique.[1] I checked the implications of the capabilities approach by "taking up particular cases in which the results of employing the [approach] can be seen in a rather stark way, and then [examined] these implications against our intuition."[2]

This project was one designed to gain insight into how we might go about promoting a society of equals. The capabilities approach brings us closer to that ideal, but I am afraid that it fails in many respects to promote justice for people with disabilities. Ignoring disability is not an option. Calling attention to injustices that run rampant in our current society can only serve to improve the process of promoting equality for not only, but principally, people with disabilities.

All in all, the arguments in this book contribute to my understanding of justice (and equality more particularly) in a number of significant ways.

91

How the Experience of Disability Impacts Justice Considerations

Prior to engaging with the capabilities approach, I explored the notion of disability. More pointedly, I attempted to highlight particular features of the experience of disability that would lead us to believe an interactional approach was the correct manner with which to conceptualize disability. I suggested that the divide present in disability theorizing was not only conceptual, but perhaps rooted in differences in discipline as well. I suggested that those theorists from the UK, typically studying sociology, have argued that the British social model is the only effective means of understanding and advocating on behalf of people with disabilities.

Conversely, I suggested that many bioethicists and philosophers, typically from North America (and also Scandinavian and Nordic countries), have embraced an interactional approach to disability.

I then introduced some general remarks in favor of the interactional model, and presented critiques by Bickenbach, Shakespeare, and Vehmas (those critiques that I view to be the most convincing and thorough refutations of the social model of disability) again to offer clarification for the reader. I then teased out further subtleties associated with the debate to further demonstrate why the criticisms from British social model theorists ought not to be taken seriously.

Only after having articulated what the experience of disability entailed did I feel I could begin to utilize that experience as a case study to highlight general inadequacies within the capabilities approach's framework.

It became overwhelmingly obvious that justice considerations must take into account both the personal and social aspects of the experience of disability. Any conception of justice that omitted either of these essential aspects of disability would invariably be inadequate.

How Disability Complicates the Assessment of Need When Attempting to Promote Equality

I reasoned that a proper conception of justice ought to have at least two mandates. The first is the identification of injustice. How one goes about initiating the second aspect, the rectification of that injustice, is another question altogether. I think it goes without saying that a failure to address the first question necessarily leads to a failure to address the second. This is why the distinction I make between horizontal-spectral analysis and vertical-spectral analysis is of utmost importance. This distinction gets to the root of the first question and suggests a capabilities approach, as conceived by Nussbaum at any rate, is unable to fulfill the requirements of the first mandate of justice.

More specifically, I launched a critique that involved a distinction I made between the performing of a horizontal spectral analysis (the ordering of a capability among other capabilities) and the performing of a vertical spectral analysis (the assessment of the opportunity or ability to achieve, secure, or perform a particular capability distinct from considerations of the relationship to other capabilities).

In making this distinction I highlighted and endorsed an analogy put forth by Wolff and De-Shalit. I pointed to their book *Disadvantage*, where they acknowledged the necessity of ranking the various capabilities and endorsed the employment of a mechanism they referred to as "complex evaluation" to provide a more robust classification of well-being. This is where their analogy gained its traction. Wolff and De-Shalit cited decathlon scoring as a prime example of how to weigh seemingly different events to arrive at a singular conclusion about an individual's overall performance. In the case of a decathlon, the performance being evaluated is, of course, an individual's athletic ability. In the case of capabilities, the evaluation is being made about an individual's well-being. That said, the importance of the analogy was in its presentation of how we might weigh seemingly incommensurable factors in coming to a solitary conclusion—a task that both decathlon scoring and the measurement of well-being within a capabilities framework must successfully perform.

I elaborated upon Wolff and De-Shalit's discussion concerning the decathlon analogy and agreed with their astute observation that first, we might be capable of measuring well-being through a complex system of evaluation. Second, I supported their claim that we must arrive at at least a partial ranking of capabilities.

I then employed their decathlon analogy to develop the distinction between horizontal spectral analysis and vertical spectral analysis. I referred to the ordering of capabilities as the horizontal spectral analysis—the ranking of capabilities among other capabilities. The primary claim made in this section, however, involved the measurement of particular functionings. I asserted that the decathlon analogy could also assist us in examining this aspect of capability theory. I called this assessment the vertical spectral analysis—the assessment of the opportunity or ability to achieve, secure, or perform a particular capability, distinct from considerations of the relationship to other capabilities. I suggested that an adequate measurement of particular capabilities required the factoring in of the social variations that impede our ability to properly situate individuals above or below a fundamental threshold.

I put forth an argument suggesting the capabilities approach was unable to properly take these social variations into account, and as such, failed to adequately perform a vertical spectral analysis. Through examining the experience of disability, I argued that our inability to properly complete this analysis was a primary problem associated with the capabilities perspective.

How the Well-Being of People With Disabilities Is Put at Risk When Identifying and Rectifying Need

After exploring the inability of the capabilities approach to properly assess need, I began to explore the further subtleties associated with how conceptions of justice identify and aim to rectify the situations of the less well-off. Referring back to the mandates of justice mentioned above, we can say that I began to examine the second mandate of a theory of justice: the rectification of that injustice. I suggested previously that a failure to satisfactorily meet the requirements of the first mandate necessarily implied a failure to meet those required to satisfy the second. While I believe this to be true, I nonetheless put this belief aside to examine how the capabilities approach would begin to address and rectify need were it capable of identifying it in the first place. What followed was an examination of the complex relationship between the identification of need, and the rectification of injustices suffered as a result of that need. I did this by taking a closer look at critiques launched by Thomas Pogge against Nussbaum, as well as the response given from Elizabeth Anderson in support of the capabilities approach.

We saw that Pogge suggested the capabilities approach stigmatized individuals in both the assessment of need and provision of resources and accommodation, thus undermining an essential aspect of one's human dignity.

I furthered this discussion by arguing that one of the primary measures of the success or failure of a conception of egalitarian justice ought to be its ability to avoid the further stigmatization of vulnerable populations. I referred to the ability to not further stigmatize individuals on the basis of naturally acquired skills or endowments as stigma-sensitivity. I concluded that despite the clear strengths of the capabilities approach, it failed to be as stigma-sensitive as alternative conceptions. I suggested that it introduced, unnecessarily, the potential to stigmatize individuals on the basis of naturally acquired skills or endowments.

In examining the claims made by Pogge, I addressed both his explicit and his implicit critique of the capabilities approach. I responded in part to these critiques by appealing to the writings of Elizabeth Anderson. I then put forth an observation of my own to address what I viewed to be an outstanding criticism emerging from Pogge's understanding. I concluded by suggesting that the capabilities approach was, by its very design, prone to being less stigma-sensitive than numerous other conceptualizations of justice.

In short, when examining competing claims of justice, attention ought to be paid to how we might begin to operationalize redistributive measures and assess need in a society where values of equality and justice are endorsed. I made a modest and I think, self-evident claim that, when comparing two equally desirable conceptions of justice, priority ought to be given to the conceptualization that is more stigma-sensitive—that stigmatizes those in need less than other, competing claims. I then went on to defend the more ambitious claim, that strict opportunity-based accounts of distributive justice increased the likelihood of further marginalizing individuals on the basis of naturally acquired skills or endowments.

How Some Capabilities Should Receive Priority as a Matter of Justice

I would then return to the notion of a horizontal spectral analysis by placing an emphasis on health. I asserted, much like Norman Daniels before me, that a conception of justice must acknowledge the special moral importance of health. I used Daniels's conception of health justice as the starting point in examining how the capabilities approach might go about addressing topics of justice and health.

I argued against Nussbaum and suggested that a focus on disadvantage can begin to satisfactorily explain why health ought to receive special moral importance. I suggested that a more nuanced recognition of Sen's notion of "basic capabilities" could get us closer to adequately characterizing how health stands in relation to other capabilities.

I argued that there are in fact, at least two classifications of capabilities. The first are capabilities whose absence results in corrosive disadvantage—in one having other capabilities put at risk. The second kind of capabilities are ones that citizens ought to have the opportunity to pursue, but whose absence do not produce corrosive disadvantage (indeed, the absence of some might not result in any kind of disadvantage whatsoever).

Concluding Remarks

The impetus to gain further insight into questions about disability and justice came from a very simple observation: equality has a long tradition in law—it is explicitly defended in the constitutions of some countries and is accepted in others still as fundamental to the notion of governance. As mentioned at the outset, I think one who asks questions about the demands of equality assumes that certain basic problems are bound to occur and seeks to address the way in which rules are developed, applied, and enforced, and how institutions, rights, and duties are organized. The notion of equality has been used as an organizing framework, at least nominally, to recognize that groups possess different natural endowments and thus are disproportionately impacted by the nature of social structures and that it is the responsibility of the state to address those issues.

Furthermore, inequality has been accepted as a recurring social, legal, and moral problem. In 2007, The *UN Convention on the Rights of Persons with Disabilities* was ratified. While it mentions the equality of opportunity as well as practices of nondiscrimination, it failed to make explicit how we should conceptualize and apply the notion of equality in greater detail.

The issues that arise from an examination of equality are not just how it has been expressed or guaranteed in or through constitutions, but the use in both case law and black-letter law to spell out the way in which people can be treated unequally within the construction of the notion of equality.

There has been little reluctance in law to accept the general principle of equality in a limited sense of formal equality, but in those cases, not unexpectedly, the courts find that there are relevant factual differences on which to base dissimilar treatment, without the principle of equality being broached. The values and assumptions around disability are often still clearly grounded in presumptions about disability as an individual pathology—as residing in the individual and not as a consequence of the political, social and economic conditions.

It is this observation—the observation that involves the importance equality has been given in grounding the rights of citizens and marginalization groups—that motivates this project.

It is our failure to theorize seriously about people with disabilities and equality that is troubling. After all, we have formal national and international documents designed to regulate the types of inequalities that are permissible. We have these documents in spite of the fact that we have neglected to properly deliberate about the intricacies associated with our conceptualization of equality. We have enacted legal and political structures to guarantee equality rights, while only having a vague notion of what we mean when we talk about equality.

This difficulty is only compounded when we examine our failure to properly deliberate about preciously what the experience of disability entails. It is no wonder the tremendous inequality currently experienced by people with disabilities is present when we consider our failure to properly deliberate about the origins of the disadvantage suffered by the disabled and the aspects of the concept of equality we aim to promote.

This very simple observation sits at the heart of the motivation to pursue this project and imparts what I view to be, the value associated with it. It is only after we have accurately taken into account precisely what it is that the experience of disability entails, and used this notion to create our conceptual understanding of equality, that we can begin to endorse the justice for people with disabilities that our social, political, and legal institutions aim to promote.

Notes

1. Amartya Sen, "Equality of What?," in *Equal Freedom: Selected Tanner Lectures on Human Values,* edited by S. Darwall (Ann Arbor: University of Michigan Press, 1995), 307.

2. Sen, "Equality of What?," 307.

Bibliography

Americans with Disabilities Act of 1990 (ADA), 42 U.S.C. §§ 12101-12213 (2000).

Anand, Paul, C. Santos, and R. Smith. "The Measurement of Capabilities." In *Arguments for a Better World: Essays in Honor of Amartya Sen*, ed. K Basu and R. Kanbur, 283–310. Oxford: Oxford University Press, 2009.

Anand, Paul, G. Hunter, I. Carter, K. Dowding, and Martin van Hees. "The Development of Capability Indicators." *Journal of Human Development and Capabilities* 10, no. 1 (2009): 125–52.

Anand, Paul, and Martin van Hees. "Capabilities and Achievements: An Empirical Study." *The Journal of Socio-Economics* 35, no. 2 (2006): 268–84.

Anderson, Elizabeth. "Justifying the Capabilities Approach to Justice." In *Measuring Justice: Primary Good and Capabilities*, ed. Harry Brighouse and Ingrid Robeyns, 81–100. Cambridge: Cambridge University Press, 2010.

———."What is the Point of Equality?." *Ethics* 109, no. 2 (1999): 287–337.

Arneson, Richard. "'Good Enough' is not Good Enough." In *Capabilities Equality: Basic Issues and Problems*, edited by Alexander Kauffman, 101–28. New York: Routledge, 2005.

———. "Equality and Equality of Opportunity for Welfare." *Philosophical Studies* 56, no. 1 (1989): 77–93.

Barnes, Colin. Review of *Arguing About Disability: Philosophical Perspectives*, ed. Kristjana Kristiansen, Simo Vehmas, and Tom Shakespeare. *Disability & Society* 25 no. 1, (2010): 123–25.

Becker, Lawrence C. *Habilitation, Health, and Agency*. Oxford: Oxford University Press, 2012.

Bickenbach, Jerome E. *Ethics, Law, and Policy*. New York: Sage Publications, 2012.

———. "Measuring Health: The Disability Critique Revisited." Paper presented at the *Third Annual International Conference on Ethical issues in the Measurement of Health and the Global Burden of Disease*. Cambridge, Massachusetts: Harvard University School of Public Health, April 24–25, 2008.

———. Review of *Distributive Justice and Disability: Utilitarianism Against Egalitarianism*, by Mark S. Stein. *Perspectives on Politics,* 5 no. 3 (2007): 621–22.

———. *Physical Disability and Social Policy*. Toronto: University of Toronto Press, 1993.

Bickenbach, Jerome E., Somnath Chatterji, E. M. Badley, and T. B. Üstün. "Models of Disablement, Universalism, and the International Classification of Impairments, Disabilities and Handicaps." *Social Science and Medicine* 48, no. 1 (1999): 1173–87.

Bukowski, Charles. *Ham on Rye*. California: Black Sparrow Press, 1982.

———. *Love is a Dog From Hell*. California: Black Sparrow Press, 1977.

Cohen, G. A. "On the Currency of Egalitarian Justice." *Ethics* 99, no. 4 (1989): 906–44.

Daniels, Norman. *Just Health: Meeting Health Needs Fairly*. New York: Cambridge University Press, 2008.

———. "Justice, Health, and Health Care." *American Journal of Bioethics* 1, no. 2 (2001): 2–16.

———. *Justice and Justification: Reflective Equilibrium in Theory and Practice*. New York: Cambridge University Press, 1999.

———. *Just Health Care*. New York: Cambridge University Press, 1985.

Dworkin, Ronald. *Sovereign Virtue: The Theory and Practice of Equality*. Cambridge: Harvard University Press, 2000.

———. "What is Equality? Part 1: Equality of Welfare." *Philosophy and Public Affairs* 10, no. 3 (1981): 185–236.

———. "What is Equality? Part 2: Equality of Resources." *Philosophy and Public Affairs* 10, no. 4 (1981): 283–345.

Harris, John. "Is There a Coherent Social Conception of Disability?" *Journal of Medical Ethics* 26, no. 2 (2000): 95–100.

Knight, Carl. "In Defence of Luck Egalitarianism." *Res Publica* 11, no. 1 (2005): 55–77.

Kuklys, Wiebke. *Amartya Sen's Capability Approach: Theoretical Insights and Empirical Applications*. Berlin: Springer-Verlag, 2005.

Macklin, Ruth. "Dignity is a Useless Concept." *British Medical Journal* 237, no. 7429 (2003): 1419–20.

Minow, Martha. *Making All the Difference: Inclusion, Exclusion, and American Law*. Ithaca: Cornell University Press, 1990.

Nibert, David Alan, Sally Cooper, and Maureen Crossmaker. "Assaults against Residents of a Psychiatric Institution: Residents' History of Abuse." *Journal of Interpersonal Violence* 4, no. 3 (1989): 342–349.

Nozick, Robert. *Anarchy, State & Utopia*. New York: Basic Books, 1974.

Nussbaum, Martha. *Creating Capabilities: The Human Development Approach*. Cambridge: The Belknap Press of Harvard University Press, 2011.

———. *Frontiers of Justice: Disability, Nationality and Species Membership*. Cambridge: The Belknap Press of Harvard University Press, 2006.

——. *Women and Human Development.* Cambridge: Cambridge University Press, 2000.

——. "Aristotelian Social Democracy." In *Liberalism and the Good,* ed. R. Bruce Douglas, Gerald M. Mara, and Henry S. Richardson, 203–52. New York: Routledge, 1990.

Oliver, Michael. Review of *Disability Rights and Wrongs,* by Tom Shakespeare. *Disability & Society* 22, no. 2 (2007): 230–4.

——. *Understanding Disability: From Theory to Practice.* New York: Saint Martin's Press, 1996.

Pogge, Thomas. "A Critique of the Capability Approach." In *Measuring Justice: Primary Good and Capabilities,* ed. Harry Brighouse and Ingrid Robeyns, 17–60. Cambridge: Cambridge University Press, 2010.

——. "Can the Capability Approach be Justified?" *Philosophical Topics* 30, no. 2 (2002): 167–228.

Rawls, John. *Political Liberalism.* New York: Columbia University Press, 1993.

——. *A Theory of Justice.* Cambridge: Harvard University Press, 1971.

Riddle, C. A. (2013). "Well-Being and the Capability of Health." *Topoi,* 32, no. 2 (2013): 153–160.

——. (2013) "Defining Disability: Metaphysical Not Political." *Medicine, Health Care, & Philosophy* 16, no. 3 (2013): 377–384.

——. (2013). "Natural Diversity and Justice for People with Disabilities." In *Disability and the Good Human Life,* edited by B. Schmitz, J. Bickenbach, and F. Felder, 269–297. Cambridge: Cambridge University Press.

——. (2013). "The Ontology of Impairment: Rethinking How We Define Disability." In *Disability Studies: Critical Issues and Future Developments,* edited by Matthew Wappett and Katrina Arndt, 23–39. New York: Palgrave Macmillian.

——. "Equality & Disability: A Charter Analysis." *Disability Studies Quarterly* 32, no. 1 (2012).

——. "Measuring Capabilities: The Case of Disability." In *The Capability Approach on Social Order,* edited by Niels Weidtmann, Yanti Martina Hölzchen, and Bilal Hawa (preface by Martha Nussbaum), 49–62. Munster: LIT Verlag, 2012.

——. "Responsibility and Foundational Material Conditions." *The American Journal of Bioethics* 11, no. 7 (2011): 53–55.

——. "Indexing, Capabilities, and Disability." *The Journal of Social Philosophy* 41, no. 4 (2010): 527–537.

Rioux, Marcia. "Disability: The Place of Judgement in a World of Fact." *Journal of Intellectual Disability Research* 41, no. 2 (1997): 102–11.

Rioux M. H., and Riddle, C. A. "Values in Disability Policy & Law: Equality." In *Critical Perspectives On Human Rights and Disability Law*, edited by M. Rioux, L. Basser, and M. Jones, 37–55. The Hague: Brill/Martinus Nijhoff Publishers, 2011.

Ruger, Jennifer Prah. *Health and Social Justice*. New York: Oxford University Press, 2009.

———. "Toward a Theory of a Right to Health: Capability and Incompletely Theorized Agreements." *Yale Journal of Law and Humanities* 17, no. 2 (2006): 273–326.

Scanlon, T. M. "Justice, Responsibility, and the Demands of Equality." In *The Egalitarian Conscience: Essays in Honour of G. A. Cohen*, edited by Christine Sypnowich, 70–87. Oxford: Oxford University Press, 2006.

Schroder, Doris. "Dignity: Two Riddles and Four Concepts." *Cambridge Quarterly of Healthcare Ethics* 17, no. 2 (2008): 230–8.

Schüklenk, Udo, and Anna Pacholczyk. "Dignity's Wooly Uplift." *Bioethics* 24, no. 2 (2010): ii.

Sen, Amartya. *Commodities and Capabilities*. India: Oxford India Paperbacks, 1999.

———. "Equality of What?" In *Equal Freedom: Selected Tanner Lectures on Human Values*, edited by S. Darwall, 307–30. Ann Arbor: University of Michigan Press, 1995).

———. "Capability and Well-Being." In *The Quality of Life*, ed. Martha Nussbaum and Amartya Sen, 30–53. Oxford: Oxford University, 1993.

———. *Inequality Reexamined*. Cambridge: Oxford University Press, 1992.

———. *On Economic Inequality*. New York: Oxford University Press, 1973.

Shakespeare, Tom. *Disability Rights and Wrongs*. New York: Routledge, 2006.

Statistics Canada, Centre for Justice Statistics, "Wife Assault: The Findings of a National Survey," *Juristate: Service Bulletin* 14, no. 9 (1994).

Stein, Mark. *Distributive Justice and Disability: Utilitarianism Against Egalitarianism*. New Haven: Yale University Press, 2006.

Terzi, Lorella. "Beyond the Dilemma of Difference: The Capability Approach to Disability and Special Educational Needs." *Journal of Philosophy of Education* 39, no. 3 (2005): 443–59.

Tremain, Shelly. "Dworkin on Disablement and Resources." *Canadian Journal of Law and Jurisprudence* 9, no. 2 (1996): 343–59.

Union of the Physically Impaired Against Segregation, *Fundament Principles of Disability*. London: Union of the Physically Impaired Against Segregation, 1976.

Vehmas, Simo and Pekka Makela. "The Ontology of Disability & Impairment: A Discussion of the Natural and Social Features." In *Arguing about Disability: Philosophical Perspectives*, ed. Kristjana Kristiansen, Simo Vehmas, and Tom Shakespeare, 42–56. London: Routledge, 2008.

———. "A Realist Account of the Ontology of Impairment." *Journal of Medical Ethics* 34, no. 2 (2008): 93–95.

Vehmas, Simo. "Philosophy and Science: The Axis of Evil in Disability Studies." *Journal of Medical Ethics*, 34 no. 1 (2008): 21–23.

———. "Dimensions of Disability." *Cambridge Quarterly of Healthcare Ethics* 13, no. 1 (2004): 34–40.

———. *Deviance, Difference and Human Variety: The Moral Significance of Disability in Modern Bioethics*. Turku: Turun Yliopisto, 2002.

Venkatapuram, Sridhar. *Health Justice: An Argument from the Capabilities Approach*. Cambridge: Polity Press, 2011.

Williams, Bernard. "The Idea of Equality." In *Philosophy, Politics, and Society (Second Series)*, ed. Peter Laslett and W. G. Runciman, 110–31. Oxford: Oxford University Press, 1969.

Wolff, Jonathan. "Disability Among Equals." In *Disability & Disadvantage*, edited by Kimberly Brownlee and Adam Cureton, 112-37. Oxford: Oxford University Press, 2009.

Wolff, Jonathan, and Avner De-Shalit. *Disadvantage*. Oxford: Oxford University Press, 2007.

World Health Organization. *World Report on Disability*. Geneva: World Health Organization, 2011.

———. *International Classification of Functioning, Disability and Health*. Geneva: World Health Organization, 2001.

———. *International Classification of Impairments, Disability, and Handicaps*. Geneva: World Health Organization, 1980.

———. Preamble to the Constitution of the World Health Organization as adopted by the International Health Conference, New York, 19 June–22 July 1946; signed on 22 July 1946 by the representatives of 61 States (Official Records of the World Health Organization, no. 2, p. 100).

Index

About the Author

Christopher A. Riddle is an Assistant Professor and Chair in the Department of Philosophy at Utica College, New York, where he is also the Director of the Applied Ethics Institute. He has taught at Concordia University in Montreal and Queen's University at Kingston, where he received his PhD.

His publications include articles in *The Journal of Social Philosophy*; *The American Journal of Bioethics*; *Medicine, Healthcare, & Philosophy*; *Topoi*; and *Disability Studies Quarterly*.

DATE DUE	RETURNED